Science and Technology

interactive
SCIENCE

PEARSON

Boston, Massachusetts
Chandler, Arizona
Glenview, Illinois
Upper Saddle River, New Jersey

AUTHORS

You're an author!

As you write in this science book, your answers and personal discoveries will be recorded for you to keep, making this book unique to you. That is why you are one of the primary authors of this book.

✎ **In the space below, print your name, school, town, and state. Then write a short autobiography that includes your interests and accomplishments.**

YOUR NAME

SCHOOL

TOWN, STATE

AUTOBIOGRAPHY

Your Photo

Acknowledgments appear on pages 163–164, which constitute an extension of this copyright page.

ISBN-13: 978-0-13-368483-4
ISBN-10: 0-13-368483-0
7 8 9 10 V011 16 15 14 13

ON THE COVER
Modeling the Internet
This model shows how all known networks connect to each other through the Internet. Each dot represents a network. The big dots in the center represent the networks that handle the most Internet traffic. Whether you connect to a central network or one of the smaller ones around the edge, you can reach anyone on any other network—worldwide!

Program Authors

DON BUCKLEY, M.Sc.
Information and Communications Technology Director, The School at Columbia University, New York, New York
Mr. Buckley has been at the forefront of K–12 educational technology for nearly two decades. A founder of New York City Independent School Technologists (NYCIST) and long-time chair of New York Association of Independent Schools' annual IT conference, he has taught students on two continents and created multimedia and Internet-based instructional systems for schools worldwide.

ZIPPORAH MILLER, M.A.Ed.
Associate Executive Director for Professional Programs and Conferences, National Science Teachers Association, Arlington, Virginia
Associate executive director for professional programs and conferences at NSTA, Ms. Zipporah Miller is a former K–12 science supervisor and STEM coordinator for the Prince George's County Public School District in Maryland. She is a science education consultant who has overseen curriculum development and staff training for more than 150 district science coordinators.

MICHAEL J. PADILLA, Ph.D.
Associate Dean and Director, Eugene P. Moore School of Education, Clemson University, Clemson, South Carolina
A former middle school teacher and a leader in middle school science education, Dr. Michael Padilla has served as president of the National Science Teachers Association and as a writer of the National Science Education Standards. He is professor of science education at Clemson University. As lead author of the *Science Explorer* series, Dr. Padilla has inspired the team in developing a program that promotes student inquiry and meets the needs of today's students.

KATHRYN THORNTON, Ph.D.
Professor and Associate Dean, School of Engineering and Applied Science, University of Virginia, Charlottesville, Virginia
Selected by NASA in May 1984, Dr. Kathryn Thornton is a veteran of four space flights. She has logged over 975 hours in space, including more than 21 hours of extravehicular activity. As an author on the *Scott Foresman Science* series, Dr. Thornton's enthusiasm for science has inspired teachers around the globe.

MICHAEL E. WYSESSION, Ph.D.
Associate Professor of Earth and Planetary Science, Washington University, St. Louis, Missouri
An author on more than 50 scientific publications, Dr. Wysession was awarded the prestigious Packard Foundation Fellowship and Presidential Faculty Fellowship for his research in geophysics. Dr. Wysession is an expert on Earth's inner structure and has mapped various regions of Earth using seismic tomography. He is known internationally for his work in geoscience education and outreach.

Instructional Design Author

GRANT WIGGINS, Ed.D.
President, Authentic Education, Hopewell, New Jersey
Dr. Wiggins is a co-author with Jay McTighe of *Understanding by Design, 2nd Edition* (ASCD 2005). His approach to instructional design provides teachers with a disciplined way of thinking about curriculum design, assessment, and instruction that moves teaching from covering content to ensuring understanding.

UNDERSTANDING BY DESIGN® and UbD™ are trademarks of ASCD, and are used under license.

Planet Diary Author

JACK HANKIN
Science/Mathematics Teacher, The Hilldale School, Daly City, California Founder, Planet Diary Web site
Mr. Hankin is the creator and writer of Planet Diary, a science current events Web site. He is passionate about bringing science news and environmental awareness into classrooms and offers numerous Planet Diary workshops at NSTA and other events to train middle and high school teachers.

ELL Consultant

JIM CUMMINS, Ph.D.
Professor and Canada Research Chair, Curriculum, Teaching and Learning department at the University of Toronto
Dr. Cummins focuses on literacy development in multilingual schools and the role of technology in promoting student learning across the curriculum. *Interactive Science* incorporates essential research-based principles for integrating language with the teaching of academic content based on his instructional framework.

Reading Consultant

HARVEY DANIELS, Ph.D.
Professor of Secondary Education, University of New Mexico, Albuquerque, New Mexico
Dr. Daniels is an international consultant to schools, districts, and educational agencies. He has authored or coauthored 13 books on language, literacy, and education. His most recent works are *Comprehension and Collaboration: Inquiry Circles in Action* and *Subjects Matter: Every Teacher's Guide to Content-Area Reading*.

REVIEWERS

Contributing Writers

Edward Aguado, Ph.D.
Professor, Department of Geography
San Diego State University
San Diego, California

Elizabeth Coolidge-Stolz, M.D.
Medical Writer
North Reading, Massachusetts

Donald L. Cronkite, Ph.D.
Professor of Biology
Hope College
Holland, Michigan

Jan Jenner, Ph.D.
Science Writer
Talladega, Alabama

Linda Cronin Jones, Ph.D.
Associate Professor of Science and Environmental Education
University of Florida
Gainesville, Florida

T. Griffith Jones, Ph.D.
Clinical Associate Professor of Science Education
College of Education
University of Florida
Gainesville, Florida

Andrew C. Kemp, Ph.D.
Teacher
Jefferson County Public Schools
Louisville, Kentucky

Matthew Stoneking, Ph.D.
Associate Professor of Physics
Lawrence University
Appleton, Wisconsin

R. Bruce Ward, Ed.D.
Senior Research Associate
Science Education Department
Harvard-Smithsonian Center for Astrophysics
Cambridge, Massachusetts

Museum of Science.

Special thanks to the Museum of Science, Boston, Massachusetts, and Ioannis Miaoulis, the Museum's president and director, for serving as content advisors for the technology and design strand in this program.

Content Reviewers

Paul D. Beale, Ph.D.
Department of Physics
University of Colorado at Boulder
Boulder, Colorado

Jeff R. Bodart, Ph.D.
Professor of Physical Sciences
Chipola College
Marianna, Florida

Joy Branlund, Ph.D.
Department of Earth Science
Southwestern Illinois College
Granite City, Illinois

Marguerite Brickman, Ph.D.
Division of Biological Sciences
University of Georgia
Athens, Georgia

Bonnie J. Brunkhorst, Ph.D.
Science Education and Geological Sciences
California State University
San Bernardino, California

Michael Castellani, Ph.D.
Department of Chemistry
Marshall University
Huntington, West Virginia

Charles C. Curtis, Ph.D.
Research Associate Professor of Physics
University of Arizona
Tucson, Arizona

Diane I. Doser, Ph.D.
Department of Geological Sciences
University of Texas
El Paso, Texas

Rick Duhrkopf, Ph.D.
Department of Biology
Baylor University
Waco, Texas

Alice K. Hankla, Ph.D.
The Galloway School
Atlanta, Georgia

Mark Henriksen, Ph.D.
Physics Department
University of Maryland
Baltimore, Maryland

Chad Hershock, Ph.D.
Center for Research on Learning and Teaching
University of Michigan
Ann Arbor, Michigan

Jeremiah N. Jarrett, Ph.D.
Department of Biology
Central Connecticut State University
New Britain, Connecticut

Scott L. Kight, Ph.D.
Department of Biology
Montclair State University
Montclair, New Jersey

Jennifer O. Liang, Ph.D.
Department of Biology
University of Minnesota–Duluth
Duluth, Minnesota

Candace Lutzow-Felling, Ph.D.
Director of Education
The State Arboretum of Virginia
University of Virginia
Boyce, Virginia

Cortney V. Martin, Ph.D.
Virginia Polytechnic Institute
Blacksburg, Virginia

Joseph F. McCullough, Ph.D.
Physics Program Chair
Cabrillo College
Aptos, California

Heather Mernitz, Ph.D.
Department of Physical Science
Alverno College
Milwaukee, Wisconsin

Sadredin C. Moosavi, Ph.D.
Department of Earth and Environmental Sciences
Tulane University
New Orleans, Louisiana

David L. Reid, Ph.D.
Department of Biology
Blackburn College
Carlinville, Illinois

Scott M. Rochette, Ph.D.
Department of the Earth Sciences
SUNY College at Brockport
Brockport, New York

Karyn L. Rogers, Ph.D.
Department of Geological Sciences
University of Missouri
Columbia, Missouri

Laurence Rosenhein, Ph.D.
Department of Chemistry
Indiana State University
Terre Haute, Indiana

Sara Seager, Ph.D.
Department of Planetary Sciences and Physics
Massachusetts Institute of Technology
Cambridge, Massachusetts

Tom Shoberg, Ph.D.
Missouri University of Science and Technology
Rolla, Missouri

Patricia Simmons, Ph.D.
North Carolina State University
Raleigh, North Carolina

William H. Steinecker, Ph.D.
Research Scholar
Miami University
Oxford, Ohio

Paul R. Stoddard, Ph.D.
Department of Geology and Environmental Geosciences
Northern Illinois University
DeKalb, Illinois

John R. Villarreal, Ph.D.
Department of Chemistry
The University of Texas–Pan American
Edinburg, Texas

John R. Wagner, Ph.D.
Department of Geology
Clemson University
Clemson, South Carolina

Jerry Waldvogel, Ph.D.
Department of Biological Sciences
Clemson University
Clemson, South Carolina

Donna L. Witter, Ph.D.
Department of Geology
Kent State University
Kent, Ohio

Edward J. Zalisko, Ph.D.
Department of Biology
Blackburn College
Carlinville, Illinois

CONTENTS

CHAPTER 1

What Is Science?

The Big Question 1
How do scientists investigate the natural world?

Vocabulary Skill: Identify Related Word Forms 2
Reading Skills 3

LESSON 1

Science and the Natural World 4
Unlock the Big Question 4
Inquiry Skill: Predict 7
do the math! Create a Bar Graph 7

LESSON 2

Thinking Like a Scientist 10
Unlock the Big Question 10
Inquiry Skill: Classify 14

LESSON 3

Scientific Inquiry 18
Unlock the Big Question 18
Inquiry Skill: Control Variables 21
do the math! Read Graphs 23
Explore the Big Question 26
Answer the Big Question 26

Study Guide & Review and Assessment 28
Review the Big Question 28
Apply the Big Question 30

Science Matters 32
• When We Think We Know, But It Isn't So • Ready for a Close-Up!

 Enter the Lab zone for hands-on inquiry.

Chapter Lab Investigation:
• Directed Inquiry: Keeping Flowers Fresh
• Open Inquiry: Keeping Flowers Fresh

Inquiry Warm-Ups: • Is It Really True?
• How Keen Are Your Senses? • What's Happening?

Quick Labs: • Classifying Objects • Thinking Like a Scientist • Using Scientific Thinking • Scientific Inquiry • Theories and Laws

my science online.com

Go to MyScienceOnline.com to interact with this chapter's content. Keyword: What Is Science?

> **UNTAMED SCIENCE**
• What Is Science, Anyway?

> **PLANET DIARY**
• What Is Science?

> **INTERACTIVE ART**
• Why Make a Model? • Inquiry Diagram
• Scientific Stumbling Blocks

> **VIRTUAL LAB**
• Introduction to Virtual Lab • What Is Scientific Inquiry?

CHAPTER 2

Science, Society, and You

The Big Question 34
How do science and society affect each other?

Vocabulary Skill: Use Context to Determine
Meaning 36
Reading Skills 37

LESSON 1

Why Study Science? 38
Unlock the Big Question 38
Inquiry Skill: Pose Questions 39, 41

LESSON 2

Scientific Literacy 42
Unlock the Big Question 42
Inquiry Skill: Interpret Data 45
Explore the Big Question 47
Answer the Big Question 47

LESSON 3

Scientists and Society 48
Unlock the Big Question 48
Inquiry Skill: Predict 51

LESSON 4

Careers in Science 52
Unlock the Big Question 52
do the math! Interpret Tables 55
Inquiry Skill: Communicate 59

Study Guide & Review and Assessment 60
Review the Big Question 60
Apply the Big Question 62

Science Matters 64
• Bakelite: Molding the Future • Caffeine Causes Hallucinations!

 Enter the Lab zone for hands-on inquiry.

Chapter Lab Investigation:
• Directed Inquiry: Piecing Information Together
• Open Inquiry: Piecing Information Together

Inquiry Warm-Ups: • How Much Do You See or Hear About Science? • Posing Questions • What Do Scientists Do? • What Do Scientists Look Like?

Quick Labs: • Using Science • Scientific Literacy Survey • Analyzing Claims • Sources of Information • Light Sources • Branches of Science • Help Wanted

my science online.com

Go to MyScienceOnline.com to interact with this chapter's content. Keyword: Science, Society, and You

> **UNTAMED SCIENCE**
• Principles of Scientific Principles

> **PLANET DIARY**
• Science, Society, and You

> **INTERACTIVE ART**
• Science in the Real World • Super Scientists

> **REAL-WORLD INQUIRY**
• When Science Sparks Controversy

CONTENTS

CHAPTER 3

The Tools of Science

The Big Question 66
How is mathematics important to the work of scientists?

Vocabulary Skill: Identify Multiple Meanings 68
Reading Skills 69

LESSON 1
Measurement—A Common Language 70
Unlock the Big Question 70
Inquiry Skill: Measure 72, 73
do the math! Calculate Density 76

LESSON 2
Mathematics and Science 80
Unlock the Big Question 80
do the math! Estimation 81
Inquiry Skill: Calculate 83, 84, 85
do the math! Sample Problem 84
Explore the Big Question 86
Answer the Big Question 87

LESSON 3
Graphs in Science 88
Unlock the Big Question 88
Inquiry Skill: Predict 91

LESSON 4
Models as Tools in Science 92
Unlock the Big Question 92
Inquiry Skill: Make Models 96

LESSON 5
Safety in the Science Laboratory 100
Unlock the Big Question 100
Inquiry Skill: Observe 104

Study Guide & Review and Assessment 106
Review the Big Question 106
Apply the Big Question 108

Science Matters 110
• You Lost What?! • Smallpox on the Loose

 Enter the Lab zone for hands-on inquiry.

Chapter Lab Investigation:
• Directed Inquiry: Density Graphs
• Open Inquiry: Density Graphs

Inquiry Warm-Ups: • History of Measurement • How Many Marbles Are There? • What's in a Picture? • Scale Models • Where Is the Safety Equipment in Your School?

Quick Labs: • How Many Shoes? • Measuring Length in Metric • For Good Measure • How Close Is It? • What's a Line Graph? • Making Models • Systems • Models in Nature • Be Prepared • Just in Case

my science ONLINE.com

Go to MyScienceOnline.com to interact with this chapter's content. Keyword: The Tools of Science

UNTAMED SCIENCE
• Measuring Up

PLANET DIARY
• The Tools of Science

INTERACTIVE ART
• The Need for Numbers • Plotting a Line Graph • Modeling a System

VIRTUAL LAB
• How Are Units Useful?

Technology and Engineering

CHAPTER 4

The Big Question 112
How does technology affect society?

Vocabulary Skill: Use Context to
Determine Meaning 114
Reading Skills 115

LESSON 1
Understanding Technology 116
Unlock the Big Question 116
Inquiry Skill: Classify 118, 122

LESSON 2
Technological Design 124
Unlock the Big Question 124
Inquiry Skill: Communicate 128

LESSON 3
Technology and Society 132
Unlock the Big Question 132
Inquiry Skill: Draw Conclusions 134, 137
do the math! Interpret Data 134
Explore the Big Question 136
Answer the Big Question 136

LESSON 4
Engineering 140
Unlock the Big Question 140
Inquiry Skill: Infer 143, 145

Study Guide & Review and Assessment 146
Review the Big Question 146
Apply the Big Question 148

Science Matters 150
• Tension in All the Right Places • Engineering Solutions

Appendices, English/Spanish Glossary, Index 152

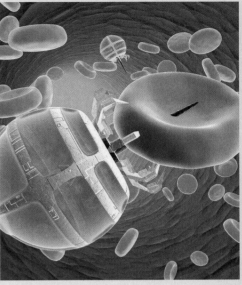

 Enter the Lab zone for hands-on inquiry.

Chapter Lab Investigation:
• Directed Inquiry: Investigating a Technological System
• Open Inquiry: Investigating a Technological System

Inquiry Warm-Ups: • What Are Some Examples of Technology? • Why Redesign? • Technology Hunt • What is Engineering?

Quick Labs: • Classifying • Processing Words • Watch Ideas Take Off • Time-Saving Technology • How Does Technology Affect Your Life? • Considering Impacts • Designing a Solution • Branches of Engineering • Advances in Transportation

MY SCIENCE online .com

Go to MyScienceOnline.com to interact with this chapter's content. Keyword: **Technology and Engineering**

> **UNTAMED SCIENCE**
• Mimicking Nature

> **PLANET DIARY**
• Technology and Engineering

> **ART IN MOTION**
• Where Did Computers Come From?

> **INTERACTIVE ART**
• Great Moments in Innovation • Evolving Technology

> **REAL-WORLD INQUIRY**
• Exploring Engineering

interactive SCIENCE

This is your book.
You can write in it!

THE BIG ?

Get Engaged!

At the start of each chapter, you will see two questions: an Engaging Question and the Big Question. Each chapter's Big Question will help you start thinking about the Big Ideas of Science. Look for the Big Q symbol throughout the chapter!

HOW CAN WIND KEEP YOUR LIGHTS ON?

THE BIG ? What are some of Earth's energy sources?

This man is repairing a wind turbine at a wind farm in Texas. Most wind turbines are at least 30 meters off the ground where the winds are fast. Wind speed and blade length help determine the best way to capture the wind and turn it into power. Develop Hypotheses Why do you think people are working to increase the amount of power we get from wind?

Wind energy collected by the turbine does not cause air pollution.

174 Energy Resources

> UNTAMED SCIENCE Watch the Untamed Science video to learn more about energy resources.

Untamed Science™

Follow the Untamed Science video crew as they travel the globe exploring the Big Ideas of Science.

Interact with your textbook.   **Interact with inquiry.**   **Interact online.**

Energy Resources

CHAPTER 5

Build Reading, Inquiry, and Vocabulary Skills

In every lesson you will learn new ↻ Reading and ▲ Inquiry skills. These skills will help you read and think like a scientist. Vocabulary skills will help you communicate effectively and uncover the meaning of words.

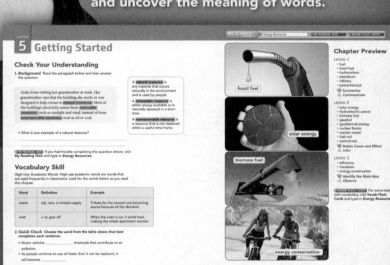

Go Online!

Look for the MyScienceOnline.com technology options. At MyScienceOnline.com you can immerse yourself in amazing virtual environments, get extra practice, and even blog about current events in science.

INTERACT... WITH YOUR TEXTBOOK...

Explore the Key Concepts.

Each lesson begins with a series of Key Concept questions. The interactivities in each lesson will help you understand these concepts and Unlock the Big Question.

MY PLANET DIARY

At the start of each lesson, My Planet Diary will introduce you to amazing events, significant people, and important discoveries in science or help you to overcome common misconceptions about science concepts.

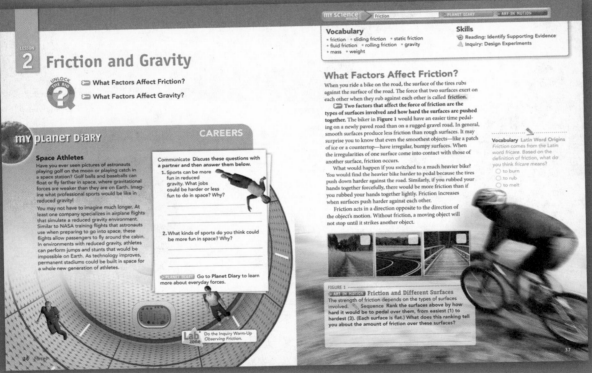

LESSON 2

Friction and Gravity

UNLOCK THE BIG ?
- What Factors Affect Friction?
- What Factors Affect Gravity?

MY PLANET DIARY

CAREERS

Space Athletes

Have you ever seen pictures of astronauts playing golf on the moon or playing catch in a space station? Golf balls and baseballs can float or fly farther in space, where gravitational forces are weaker than they are on Earth. Imagine what professional sports would be like in reduced gravity!

You may not have to imagine much longer. At least one company specializes in airplane flights that simulate a reduced gravity environment. Similar to NASA training flights that astronauts use when preparing to go into space, these flights allow passengers to fly around the cabin. In environments with reduced gravity, athletes can perform jumps and stunts that would be impossible on Earth. As technology improves, permanent stadiums could be built in space for a whole new generation of athletes.

Communicate Discuss these questions with a partner and then answer them below.

1. Sports can be more fun in reduced gravity. What jobs could be harder or less fun to do in space? Why?

2. What kinds of sports do you think could be more fun in space? Why?

> **PLANET DIARY** Go to Planet Diary to learn more about everyday forces.

Lab zone Do the Inquiry Warm-Up Observing Friction.

26 Forces

MY SCIENCE [Friction] [PLANET DIARY] [ART IN MOTION]

Vocabulary
- friction • sliding friction • static friction
- fluid friction • rolling friction • gravity
- mass • weight

Skills
- Reading: Identify Supporting Evidence
- Inquiry: Design Experiments

What Factors Affect Friction?

When you ride a bike on the road, the surface of the tires rubs against the surface of the road. The force that two surfaces exert on each other when they rub against each other is called **friction**.

Two factors that affect the force of friction are the types of surfaces involved and how hard the surfaces are pushed together. The biker in **Figure 1** would have an easier time pedaling on a newly paved road than on a rugged gravel road. In general, smooth surfaces produce less friction than rough surfaces. It may surprise you to know that even the smoothest objects—like a patch of ice or a countertop—have irregular, bumpy surfaces. When the irregularities of one surface come into contact with those of another surface, friction occurs.

What would happen if you switched to a much heavier bike? You would find the heavier bike harder to pedal because the tires push down harder against the road. Similarly, if you rubbed your hands together forcefully, there would be more friction than if you rubbed your hands together lightly. Friction increases when surfaces push harder against each other.

Friction acts in a direction opposite to the direction of the object's motion. Without friction, a moving object will not stop until it strikes another object.

Vocabulary Latin Word Origins Friction comes from the Latin word fricare. Based on the definition of friction, what do you think fricare means?
- ○ to burn
- ○ to rub
- ○ to melt

FIGURE 1

ART IN MOTION Friction and Different Surfaces
The strength of friction depends on the types of surfaces involved. Sequence Rank the surfaces above by how hard it would be to pedal over them, from easiest (1) to hardest (3). (Each surface is flat.) What does this ranking tell you about the amount of friction over these surfaces?

37

Explain what you know.

Look for the pencil. When you see it, it's time to interact with your book and demonstrate what you have learned.

Desertification If the soil in a[...] of moisture and nutrients, the a[...] advance of desertlike conditions [...] fertile is called **desertification** [...]

One cause of desertification [...] is a period when less rain than n[...] droughts, crops fail. Without pla[...] blows away. Overgrazing of gras[...] cutting down trees for firewood [...]

Desertification is a serious p[...] and graze livestock where desert[...] people may face famine and star[...] central Africa. Millions of rural [...] cities because they can no longer [...]

apply it!

Desertification affects many areas around the world.

❶ Name Which continent has the most existing desert?

❷ Interpret Maps Where in the United States is the greatest risk of desertification?

❸ Infer Is desertification a threa[...] is existing desert? Explain. Circle your answer.

❹ CHALLENGE If an area is facing [...] things people could do to possib[...]

132 Land, Air, and Water Resou[...]

---

apply it!

Elaborate further with the Apply It activities. This is your opportunity to take what you've learned and apply those skills to new situations.

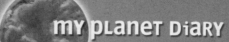

xii

Lab Zone

Look for the Lab zone triangle. This means it's time to do a hands-on inquiry lab. In every lesson, you'll have the opportunity to do a hands-on inquiry activity that will help reinforce your understanding of the lesson topic.

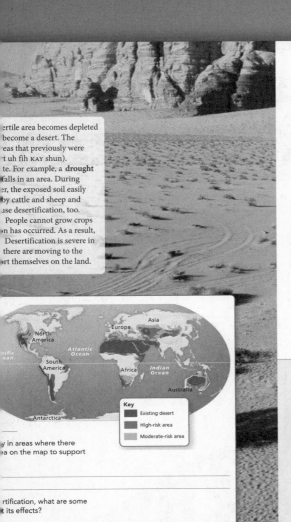

ertile area becomes depleted
become a desert. The
eas that previously were
t uh fih KAY shun).
te. For example, a **drought**
falls in an area. During
r, the exposed soil easily
by cattle and sheep and
se desertification, too.
People cannot grow crops
n has occurred. As a result,
Desertification is severe in
there are moving to the
rt themselves on the land.

Key
- Existing desert
- High-risk area
- Moderate-risk area

y in areas where there
a on the map to support

rtification, what are some
t its effects?

Land Reclamation Fortunately, it is possible to replace land damaged by erosion or mining. The process of restoring an area of land to a more productive state is called **land reclamation.** In addition to restoring land for agriculture, land reclamation can restore habitats for wildlife. Many different types of land reclamation projects are currently underway all over the world. But it is generally more difficult and expensive to restore damaged land and soil than it is to protect those resources in the first place. In some cases, the land may not return to its original state.

FIGURE 4 ·······················

Land Reclamation
These pictures show land before and after it was mined.

✏ **Communicate** Below the pictures, write a story about what happened to the land.

Assess Your Understanding

1a. Review Subsoil has (less/more) plant and animal matter than topsoil.

b. Explain What can happen to soil if plants are removed?
_____

c. Apply Concepts
that could prev
land reclama

got it? ·····························

○ I get it! Now I know that soil management is important becau

○ I need extra help with _____
Go to MY SCIENCE (S) COACH online for help with this subject.

Lab zone Do the Quick Lab
Modeling S

got it?

Evaluate Your Progress.

After answering the Got It question, think about how you're doing. Did you get it or do you need a little help? Remember, MY SCIENCE (S) COACH is there for you if you need extra help.

Explore the Big Question.

At one point in the chapter, you'll have the opportunity to take all that you've learned to further explore the Big Question.

Pollution and Solutions

What can people do to use resources wisely?

FIGURE 4 ....
▶ **REAL-WORLD INQUIRY** All living things depend on land, air, and water. Conserving these resources for the future is important. Part of resource conservation is identifying and limiting sources of pollution.

✎ **Interpret Photos** On the photograph, write the letter from the key into the circle that best identifies the source of pollution.

Land
Describe at least one thing your community could do to reduce pollution on land.
_____
_____
_____
_____
_____

Air
Describe at least one thing your community could do to reduce air pollution.
_____
_____
_____
_____
_____

Water
Describe at least one thing your community could do to reduce water pollution.
_____
_____
_____
_____
_____

Pollution Sources
A. Sediments
B. Municipal solid waste
C. Runoff from development

Lab Do
zone Ge

▭ **Assess Your Unde**

1a. Define What are sediments?
_____

b. Explain How can bacteria he
spill in the ocean?
_____

c. ANSWER What can people do
? resources wisely?
_____
_____

d. CHALLENGE Why might a co
to recycle the waste they p
would reduce water polluti
_____
_____
_____
_____

got it? ....
○ I get it! Now I know that
can be reduced by _____

○ I need extra help with _____

Go to MY SCIENCE coa
with this subject.

Answer the Big Question.

Now it's time to show what you know and answer the Big Question.

Review What You've Learned.

Use the Chapter Study Guide to review the Big Question and prepare for the test.

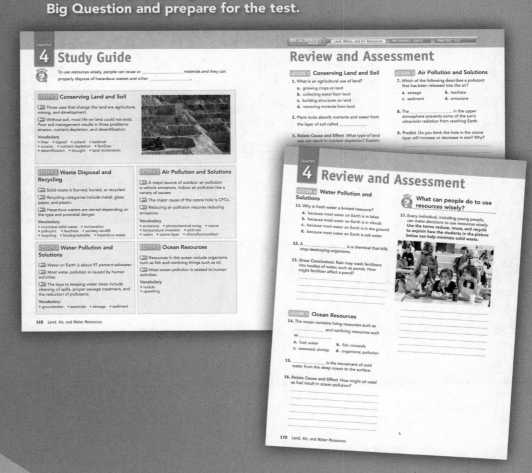

Practice Taking Tests.

Apply the Big Question and take a practice test in standardized test format.

Go to <u>MyScienceOnline.com</u> and immerse yourself in amazing virtual environments.

▶ THE BIG QUESTION

Each online chapter starts with a Big Question. Your mission is to unlock the meaning of this Big Question as each science lesson unfolds.

▶ VOCAB FLASH CARDS

Practice chapter vocabulary with interactive flash cards. Each card has an image, definitions in English and Spanish, and space for your own notes.

▶ INTERACTIVE ART

At MyScienceOnline.com, many of the beautiful visuals in your book become interactive so you can extend your learning.

GO ONLINE

⟳ | + | 🌐 http://www.myscienceonline.com/

> PLANET DIARY

My Planet Diary online is the place to find more information and activities related to the topic in the lesson.

Elaborate | Evaluate

t Everest

Still Growing! Mount Everest in the Himalayas is the highest mountain on Earth. Climbers who reach the peak stand 8,850 meters above sea level. You might think that mountains never change. But forces inside Earth push Mount Everest at least several millimeters higher each year. Over time, Earth's forces slowly but constantly lift, stretch, bend, and break Earth's crust in dramatic ways!

> Planet Diary Go to Planet Diary to learn more about forces in the Earth's crust.

Tools
123

Next
22 of 22
Back

> VIRTUAL LAB

Get more practice with realistic virtual labs. Manipulate the variables on-screen and test your hypothesis.

Find Your Chapter

1 Go to www.myscienceonline.com.

2 Log in with username and password.

3 Click on your program and select your chapter.

Keyword Search

1 Go to www.myscienceonline.com.

2 Log in with username and password.

3 Click on your program and select Search.

4 Enter the keyword (from your book) in the search box.

Other Content Available Online

> UNTAMED SCIENCE Follow these young scientists through their amazing online video blogs as they travel the globe in search of answers to the Big Questions of Science.

> MY SCIENCE COACH Need extra help? My Science Coach is your personal online study partner. My Science Coach is a chance for you to get more practice on key science concepts. There you can choose from a variety of tools that will help guide you through each science lesson.

> MY READING WEB Need extra reading help on a particular science topic? At My Reading Web you will find a choice of reading selections targeted to your specific reading level.

? BIG IDEAS OF SCIENCE

Have you ever worked on a jigsaw puzzle? Usually a puzzle has a theme that leads you to group the pieces by what they have in common. But until you put all the pieces together you can't solve the puzzle. Studying science is similar to solving a puzzle. The big ideas of science are like puzzle themes. To understand big ideas, scientists ask questions. The answers to those questions are like pieces of a puzzle. Each chapter in this book asks a big question to help you think about a big idea of science. By answering the big questions, you will get closer to understanding the big idea.

✎ **Before you read each chapter, write about what you know and what more you'd like to know.**

Grant Wiggins, co-author of *Understanding by Design, 2nd Edition*, (ASCD 2005). UNDERSTANDING BY DESIGN® and UbD™ are trademarks of ASCD, and are used under license.

Scientists use their senses to investigate the natural world. For example, a scientist could observe these chimpanzees to figure out why they are sticking a stem in the termite mound.

BIGIDEA

Scientists use scientific inquiry to explain the natural world.

What do you already know about how you study the natural world? ✎ **What more would you like to know?**

_____

_____

_____

Big Question:

? How do scientists investigate the natural world? Chapter 1

✎ **After reading the chapter, write what you have learned about the Big Idea.**

_____

_____

_____

_____

_____

_____

BIGIDEA
Science, technology, and society affect each other.

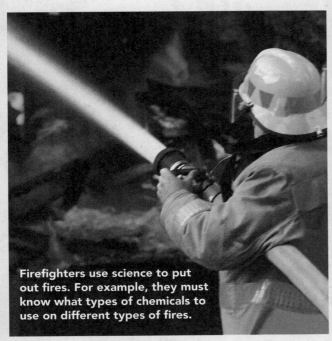

Firefighters use science to put out fires. For example, they must know what types of chemicals to use on different types of fires.

What do you already know about how science affects your everyday life? ✏ **What more would you like to know?**

_____

_____

_____

Big Questions:

❓ How do science and society affect each other? Chapter 2

❓ How does technology affect society? Chapter 4

✏ **After reading the chapters, write what you have learned about the Big Idea.**

_____

_____

_____

_____

_____

BIGIDEA
Scientists use mathematics in many ways.

Scientists rely on estimates when they cannot obtain exact data. Estimating is a quick way of determining how many birds are in this photo.

Which math skills have you used to study science? ✏ **Which math skills do you need to practice?**

_____

_____

_____

_____

Big Question:

❓ How is mathematics important to the work of scientists? Chapter 3

✏ **After reading the chapter, write what you have learned about the Big Idea.**

firefighters

_____

_____

_____

_____

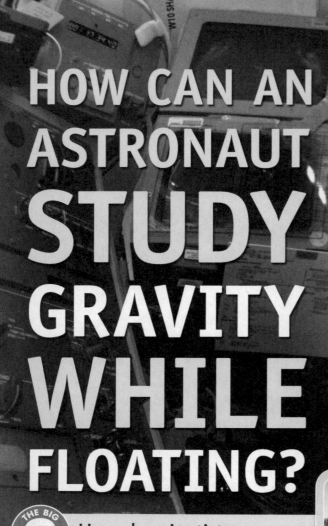

HOW CAN AN ASTRONAUT STUDY GRAVITY WHILE FLOATING?

 THE BIG Q?

How do scientists investigate the natural world?

NASA studies how microgravity, or very little gravity, affects humans, plants, crystals, and liquids. For example, NASA has found that the muscles and bones of astronauts weaken during space missions. Plants grow in different directions, crystals grow larger, and water does not pour as it would on Earth, but falls out in spheres.

▷ **Infer** What other ideas might NASA study in space?

_____

_____

_____

_____

_____

▷ **UNTAMED SCIENCE** Watch the **Untamed Science** video to learn more about science.

What Is Science?

Check Your Understanding

1. **Background** Read the paragraph below and then answer the question.

Miki is in the **process** of preparing a stew for dinner at her campsite. After it is cooked, she sets the pot aside to cool. When she returns, the pot is empty. Immediately, she **poses** questions: Who ate the stew? What animals are active in the evening? She soon finds **evidence:** the pot cover, greasy spills, and a stinky smell. The thief is a skunk.

A **process** is a series of actions or events.

To **pose** is to put forward a question or a problem.

Facts, figures, or signs that help prove a statement are all pieces of **evidence.**

• How does the process of posing questions and looking for evidence help Miki solve the mystery of the missing stew?

_____

_____

> MY READING WEB   If you had trouble completing the question above, visit **My Reading Web** and type in *What Is Science?*

Vocabulary Skill

Identify Related Word Forms Learn related forms of words to increase your vocabulary. The table below lists forms of words related to vocabulary terms.

Verb	Noun	Adjective
observe, *v.* to gather information using the senses	observation, *n.* facts learned by gathering information using the senses	observable, *adj.* able to be heard, seen, touched, tasted, or smelled
predict, *v.* to state or claim what will happen in the future	prediction, *n.* a statement or claim of what will happen in the future	predictable, *adj.* able to be predicted; behaving in a way that is expected

2. **Quick Check** Complete the sentence with the correct form of the word.

• It is difficult to _____ how much rain will fall.

observing

subjective

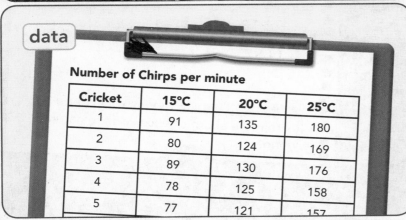

data

Number of Chirps per minute

Cricket	15°C	20°C	25°C
1	91	135	180
2	80	124	169
3	89	130	176
4	78	125	158
5	77	121	157

controlled experiment

Chapter Preview

LESSON 1
- science
- observing
- quantitative observation
- qualitative observation
- inferring
- predicting
- classifying
- evaluating
- making models

🔁 Ask Questions
△ Predict

LESSON 2
- skepticism
- ethics
- personal bias
- cultural bias
- experimental bias
- objective
- subjective
- deductive reasoning
- inductive reasoning

🔁 Relate Cause and Effect
△ Classify

LESSON 3
- scientific inquiry ✗
- hypothesis ✗
- variable ✗
- manipulated variable ✗
- responding variable ✗
- controlled experiment ✗
- data ✗
- scientific theory ✗
- scientific law ✗

🔁 Sequence
△ Control Variables

> VOCAB FLASH CARDS For extra help with vocabulary, visit **Vocab Flash Cards** and type in *What Is Science?*

Science and the Natural World

What Skills Do Scientists Use?

my planet Diary

BIOGRAPHY

The Wild Chimpanzees of Gombe

The following words are from the writings of Jane Goodall, a scientist who studied wild chimpanzees in Africa for many years.

"Once, as I walked through thick forest in a downpour, I suddenly saw a chimp hunched in front of me. Quickly I stopped. Then I heard a sound from above. I looked up and there was a big chimp there, too. When he saw me he gave a loud, clear wailing *wraaaaah*— a spine-chilling call that is used to threaten a dangerous animal. To my right I saw a large black hand shaking a branch and bright eyes glaring threateningly through the foliage. Then came another savage *wraaaah* from behind...I was surrounded." Because Jane stood still, the chimps no longer felt threatened, so they went away.

Answer the question.

What is one advantage and one disadvantage of studying wild animals in their natural environment?

They are part of our enviroment. They behave differently from us.

> PLANET DIARY Go to **Planet Diary** to learn more about science and the natural world.

Lab zone Do the Inquiry Warm-Up *Is It Really True?*

Vocabulary
- science • observing • quantitative observation
- qualitative observation • inferring • predicting
- classifying • evaluating • making models

Skills
- Reading: Ask Questions
- Inquiry: Predict

What Skills Do Scientists Use?

Jane Goodall trained herself to become a scientist, or a person who does science. **Science** is a way of learning about the natural world. Science also includes all the knowledge gained by exploring the natural world. **Scientists use skills such as observing, inferring, predicting, classifying, evaluating, and making models to study the world.**

Observing

Observing means using one or more of your senses to gather information. It also means using tools, such as a microscope, to help your senses. By observing chimps like the one in **Figure 1**, Jane Goodall learned what they eat. She also learned what sounds chimps make and even what games they play.

Observations can be either quantitative or qualitative. A **quantitative observation** deals with numbers, or amounts. For example, seeing that you have 11 new e-mails is a quantitative observation. A **qualitative observation** deals with descriptions that cannot be expressed in numbers. Noticing that a bike is blue or that a lemon tastes sour is a qualitative observation.

Ask Questions In the graphic organizer ask a *what*, *how*, or *why* question based on the text under Observing. As you read, write an answer to your question.

FIGURE 1 ·········
Observing
A chimpanzee uses a rock as a tool to crack open a nut.

✎ **Observe** Write one quantitative observation and one qualitative observation about this chimp.

This chimp has 2 Rocks

The chimp is busy looking at the rocks.

Thinking Like a Scientist

Question

How are Chimps

Answer

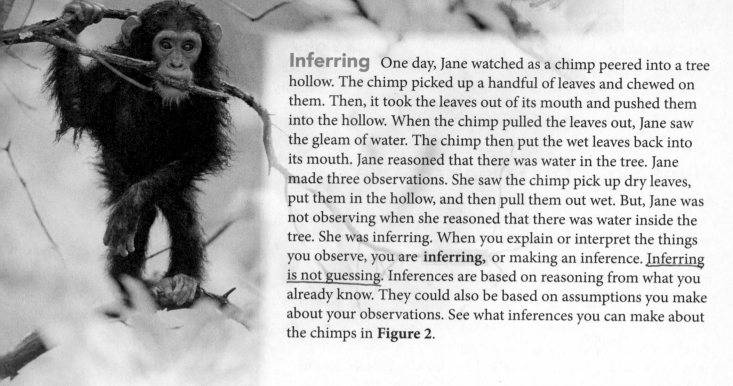

Inferring One day, Jane watched as a chimp peered into a tree hollow. The chimp picked up a handful of leaves and chewed on them. Then, it took the leaves out of its mouth and pushed them into the hollow. When the chimp pulled the leaves out, Jane saw the gleam of water. The chimp then put the wet leaves back into its mouth. Jane reasoned that there was water in the tree. Jane made three observations. She saw the chimp pick up dry leaves, put them in the hollow, and then pull them out wet. But, Jane was not observing when she reasoned that there was water inside the tree. She was inferring. When you explain or interpret the things you observe, you are **inferring,** or making an inference. Inferring is not guessing. Inferences are based on reasoning from what you already know. They could also be based on assumptions you make about your observations. See what inferences you can make about the chimps in **Figure 2.**

FIGURE 2 ···

✳Inferring
What can you infer about the chimps and the termite mound?

✎ **Complete the activities below.**

1. **Observe** In the chart below, write two observations about the chimp on the left.

2. **Infer** Use the observations you wrote to make two related inferences.

Observation	Inference
The chip on the left is busy looking at the rock. The chip on the left is using his full sences.	The two chips are both looking down. The chip's got a sunburn.

Predicting

Jane's understanding of chimp behavior grew over time. Sometimes, she could predict what a chimp would do next. **Predicting** means making a statement or a claim about what will happen in the future based on past experience or evidence.

By observing, Jane learned that when a chimp was frightened or angry its hairs stood on end. This response was sometimes followed by threatening gestures such as charging, throwing rocks, and shaking trees. Therefore, when Jane saw a chimp with its hair on end, she was able to predict that there was danger.

Predictions and inferences are closely related. While inferences are attempts to explain what is happening or *has* happened, predictions are statements or claims about what *will* happen. If you see a broken egg on the floor by a table, you might infer that the egg had rolled off the table. If, however, you see an egg rolling toward the edge of a table, you can predict that it's about to create a mess.

FIGURE 3 ·······························
Predicting
Predictions are forecasts of what will happen next.

✏ **Predict** Write a prediction about what this angry chimp might do next.

He might kill something

do the math!

Like all animals, chimps prefer to eat certain foods when they are available.

1 Graph Use the information in the table to create a bar graph.

2 Label the x-axis and the y-axis. Then write a title for the graph.

3 Interpret Data Did chimps feed more on seeds or leaves during May?

_____

_____

4 Infer What might chimps eat more of if fruits are not available in June?

_____

_____

_____

Chimp Diet in May	
Fruits	52%
Seeds	30%
Leaves	12%
Other foods	6%

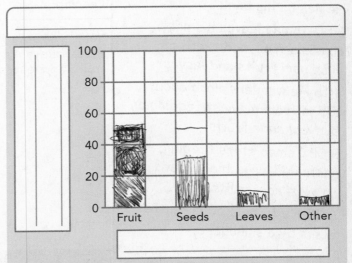

Classifying

What did chimps do all day? To find out, Jane's research team followed the chimps through the forest. They took detailed field notes about the chimps' behaviors. **Figure 4** shows some notes about Jomeo, an adult male chimp.

Suppose Jane had wanted to know how much time Jomeo spent feeding or resting that morning. She could have found out by classifying Jomeo's actions. **Classifying** is the grouping together of items that are alike in some way. Jane could have grouped together all the information about Jomeo's feeding habits or his resting behavior.

Evaluating

Suppose Jane had found that Jomeo spent most of his time resting. What would this observation have told her about chimp behavior? Before Jane could have reached a conclusion, she would have needed to evaluate her observations. **Evaluating** involves comparing observations and data to reach a conclusion about them. For example, Jane would have needed to compare all of Jomeo's behaviors with those of other chimps to reach a conclusion. She would also need to have evaluated the resulting behavior data of Jomeo and the other chimps.

FIGURE 4 ·······························

> VIRTUAL LAB **Classifying**

By classifying the information related to a chimp's resting, climbing, or feeding, a scientist can better understand chimp behavior.

✎ **Classify** Use the chart to classify the details from the field notes.

- 6:45 A.M. Jomeo rests in his nest. He lies on his back.
- 6:50 Jomeo leaves his nest, climbs a tree, and feeds on *viazi pori* fruits and leaves.
- 7:16 He wanders along about 175 m from his nest feeding on *budyankende* fruits.
- 8:08 Jomeo stops feeding, rests in a large tree, feeds on *viazi pori* fruits again.
- 8:35 He travels 50 m further, rests by a small lake.

Feeding	Resting	Changing Location
Jomeo eats *viazi pori* fruits, *budyankende* fruits, and leaves.	8:35 am his rest. 6:45am Rests	6:50 7:16 8:35

Making Models How far do chimps travel? Where do they go? Sometimes, Jane's research team followed a particular chimp for many days at a time. To show the chimp's movements, they might have made a model like the one shown in **Figure 5**. The model shows Jomeo's movements and behaviors during one day. **Making models** involves creating representations of complex objects or processes. Some models can be touched, such as a map. Others are in the form of mathematical equations or computer programs. Models help people study things that can't be observed directly. By using models, Jane and her team shared information that would otherwise be difficult to explain.

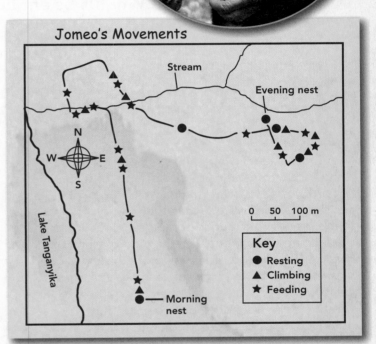

Jomeo's Movements

FIGURE 5 ....

> **INTERACTIVE ART** **Making Models**
This model shows Jomeo's movements and behaviors during one day.

✎ **Use the map to answer the questions.**

1. Interpret Maps How far did Jomeo travel during this day?

_____

_____

2. How many times did Jomeo stop to feed?

_____

3. How many times did Jomeo rest?

_____

Lake Tanganyika

Stream

Evening nest

0   50   100 m

Key
● Resting
▲ Climbing
★ Feeding

Morning nest

 Do the Quick Lab
Classifying Objects.

✗ 🔑 **Assess Your Understanding**

Compare and Contrast How do observations differ from inferences?

They are different because Observation is to Observe and Inference is to differ

Classify Do you think this statement is an observation or an inference? *The cat is ill.* Explain your reasoning.

inference. Because inference means based on assumptions you make about your observation.

got it? ....

○ **I get it!** I know that scientists use skills such as _____

_____

○ I need extra help with _____

Go to **MY SCIENCE 🔵 COACH** *online for help with this subject.*

Thinking Like a Scientist

UNLOCK THE BIG ?

🔑 **What Attitudes Help You Think Scientifically?**

🔑 **What Is Scientific Reasoning?**

MY PLANET DIARY

Incredible Inventions

Most scientific inventions are purposely created and result from curiosity, persistence, and years of hard work. However, some inventions have been accidentally discovered when their inventors were in the process of creating something else. While developing wallpaper cleaner, a type of clay was invented. A coil-shaped toy was originally designed as a spring to be used on ships. Instead of developing a substitute for synthetic rubber, toy putty was created. Self-stick notes, potato chips, and the hook and loop fasteners used on items such as clothing, shoes, and toys are also inventions that were discovered by accident. Like the inventors of these items, your curiosity may help you invent the next "big thing"!

DISCOVERY

Communicate Discuss the following questions with a partner. Write your answers below.

1. Why do you think it is important for scientists to be curious?

_____

_____

_____

2. What might you want to invent? Why?

_____

_____

_____

_____

▶ **PLANET DIARY** Go to **Planet Diary** to learn more about thinking like a scientist.

Lab zone® Do the Inquiry Warm-Up *How Keen Are Your Senses?*

Vocabulary
- skepticism • ethics • personal bias • cultural bias
- experimental bias • objective • subjective
- deductive reasoning • inductive reasoning

Skills
↺ Reading: Relate Cause and Effect
△ Inquiry: Classify

What Attitudes Help You Think Scientifically?

Perhaps someone has told you that you have a good attitude. What does that mean? An attitude is a state of mind. Your actions say a lot about your attitude. ⊂⊐ **Scientists possess certain important attitudes, including curiosity, honesty, creativity, open-mindedness, skepticism, good ethics, and awareness of bias.**

Curiosity One attitude that drives scientists is curiosity. Scientists want to learn more about the topics they study. **Figure 1** shows some things that may spark the interest of scientists.

Honesty Good scientists always report their observations and results truthfully. Honesty is especially important when a scientist's results go against previous ideas or predictions.

Creativity Whatever they study, scientists may experience problems. Sometimes, it takes creativity to find a solution. Creativity means coming up with inventive ways to solve problems or produce new things.

FIGURE 1 ·······································
Curiosity
Curiosity helps scientists learn about the world around them.

✎ **Ask Questions** For each image, write a question you are curious about in the boxes.

The hot spring is blowing up like a water sprout

frog jumping like a phaying frog

The Cloud is during into a rainbow

11

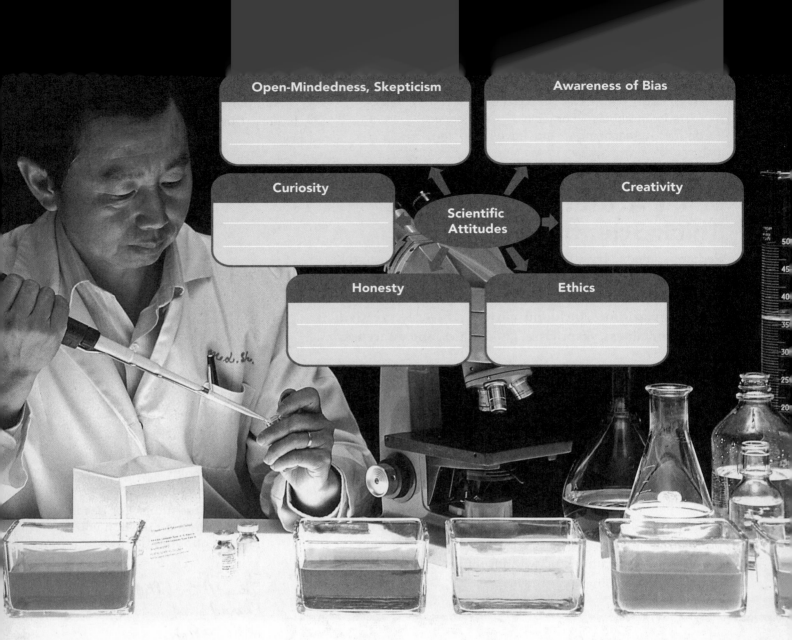

Open-Mindedness, Skepticism	Awareness of Bias
Curiosity	Scientific Attitudes	Creativity
Honesty	Ethics

FIGURE 2 ·······································
Attitudes of Scientists
This scientist is carefully conducting an experiment.

✎ **Summarize** After you have read the section What Attitudes Help You Think Scientifically?, write a summary of each scientific attitude in the graphic organizer.

Open-Mindedness and Skepticism Scientists need to be open-minded, or capable of accepting new and different ideas. However, open-mindedness should always be balanced by **skepticism,** which is having an attitude of doubt. Skepticism keeps a scientist from accepting ideas that may be untrue.

Ethics Because scientists work with the natural world, they must be careful not to damage it. Scientists need a strong sense of **ethics,** which refers to the rules that enable people to know right from wrong. Scientists must consider all the effects their research may have on people and the environment. They make decisions only after considering the risks and benefits to living things or the environment. For example, scientists test medicine they have developed before the medicine is sold to the public. Scientists inform volunteers of the new medicine's risks before allowing them to take part in the tests. Look at **Figure 2** to review scientific attitudes.

Awareness of Bias What scientists expect to find can influence, or bias, what they observe and how they interpret observations. For example, a scientist might misinterpret the behavior of an animal because of what she already knows about animals.

There are different kinds of bias. **Personal bias** comes from a person's likes and dislikes. For instance, if you like the taste of a cereal, you might think everyone else should, too. **Cultural bias** stems from the culture in which a person grows up. For example, a culture that regards snakes as bad might overlook how well snakes control pests. **Experimental bias** is a mistake in the design of an experiment that makes a particular result more likely. For example, suppose you wanted to determine the boiling point of pure water. If your experiment uses water that has some salt in it, your results would be biased.

·········· ✏ ··········

🔁 **Relate Cause and Effect**
In the first paragraph, underline an example of bias. Then circle its effect.

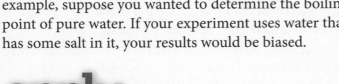

apply *it!*

Matt likes cheese crackers best and thinks that most other students do too. So he observed what students bought at the vending machine during one lunch. Seven bought crackers, three bought nuts, and none bought raisins.

1 Circle the evidence of personal bias.

2 CHALLENGE Describe the experimental bias.

_____

_____

_____

Lab zone® Do the Quick Lab *Thinking Like a Scientist.*

🔑 **Assess Your Understanding**

1a. Explain What can bias a scientist's observations?

_____

_____

b. Apply Concepts Debbie discovered a new way to make pizza. What scientific attitude is this an example of?

_____

got *it?*

○ **I get it!** Now I know that attitudes that help you think scientifically are _____

_____

_____

○ **I need extra help with** _____

Go to **MY SCIENCE** 🔵 **COACH** *online for help with this subject.*

What Is Scientific Reasoning?

You use reasoning, or a logical way of thinking, when you solve word problems. Scientists use reasoning in their work, too. **Scientific reasoning requires a logical way of thinking based on gathering and evaluating evidence.** There are two types of scientific reasoning. Scientific reasoning can be deductive or inductive.

Because scientific reasoning relies on gathering and evaluating evidence, it is objective reasoning. Being **objective** means that you make decisions and draw conclusions based on available evidence. For example, scientists used to think chimps ate only plants. However, Jane Goodall observed chimps eating meat. Based on this evidence, she concluded that chimps ate meat and plants.

In contrast, being **subjective** means that personal feelings have entered into a decision or conclusion. Personal opinions, values, and tastes are subjective because they are based on your feelings about something. For example, if you see a clear stream in the woods, you might take a drink because you think clear water is clean. However, you have not objectively tested the water's quality. The water might contain microorganisms you cannot see and be unsafe to drink.

apply it!

Classify Read the sentences below. Then decide if each example uses objective reasoning or subjective reasoning to reach a conclusion. Place a check mark in the corresponding column.

	Objective	Subjective
Jane Goodall saw a chimp chewing on wet leaves. She reasoned that chimps sometimes used leaves to drink water.		
I like to run. I must be the fastest person in the class.		
Emily is 1.2 m tall. No one else in class is taller than 1 m. So, Emily is the tallest person in class.		
I dislike dogs. Dogs must be the least friendly animals.		

Deductive Reasoning Scientists who study Earth think that the uppermost part of Earth's surface is made up of many sections they call plates. The theory of plate tectonics states that earthquakes should happen mostly where plates meet. There are many earthquakes in California. Therefore, California must be near a place where plates meet. This is an example of deductive reasoning. **Deductive reasoning** is a way to explain things by starting with a general idea and then applying the idea to a specific observation.

You can think about deductive reasoning as being a process. First, you state the general idea. Then you relate the general idea to the specific case you are investigating. Then you reach a conclusion. You can use this process in **Figure 3**. The process for the plate tectonics example is shown here.

- Earthquakes should happen mostly where plates meet.
- California has many earthquakes.
- California must be near a place where plates meet.

did you know?

Did you know that deductive reasoning is used by detectives? Sherlock Holmes, a fictional detective in the novels and short stories of Sir Arthur Conan Doyle, solved many mysteries using deductive reasoning.

FIGURE 3 ·····

Deductive Reasoning
Deductive reasoning occurs when a general idea is applied to a specific example and a conclusion is reached.

✎ **Apply Concepts** Apply each general idea to a specific example and then draw a conclusion.

Dinner is always at 6 P.M.
Not all the time

Classes end when the bell rings.
yes class can end when the bell ring

Triangles have three sides.
Always

Inductive Reasoning Scientists also use inductive reasoning, which can be considered the opposite of deductive reasoning. **Inductive reasoning** uses specific observations to make generalizations. For example, suppose you notice that leaf-cutter ants appear to follow other ants along specific paths, as shown in **Figure 4**. The ants follow the paths to sources of food, water, and nest material. Then they return to their nests. These observations about the leaf-cutter ants are specific. From these specific observations you conclude that these ants must communicate to be able to always follow the same path. This conclusion is a generalization about the behavior of leaf-cutter ants based on your observations. Scientists frequently use inductive reasoning. They collect data and then reach a conclusion based on that data.

FIGURE 4 ···

> INTERACTIVE ART **Scientific Reasoning**
Leaf-cutter ants follow a chemical trail to find and harvest leaves.

✎ **Identify Look at the statements below. Write *D* next to the statements that use deductive reasoning. Write *I* next to the statements that use inductive reasoning.**

❶ Turtles have shells. They must use shells for protection. _____

❷ A puddle has frozen. It must be below 0°C outside. _____

❸ Because of gravity, everything that goes up must come down. _____

❹ Many birds fly toward the equator in fall. Birds prefer warm weather. _____

Faulty Reasoning Scientists must be careful not to use faulty reasoning, because it can lead to faulty conclusions. If you draw a conclusion based on too little data, your reasoning might lead you to the wrong general idea. For example, to conclude accurately that all ants communicate with each other, you would have to observe leaf-cutter ants and many other kinds of ants many times. In addition, based on observations of how leaf-cutter ants follow paths, you cannot conclude how they communicated. For example, you cannot say they follow the tiny footprints of the ants ahead of them. Such a conclusion would be a guess not based on observation.

apply it!

Joy drew lines of symmetry on a square. She saw that a rectangle has four straight sides and four right angles, so she drew the same lines of symmetry on a rectangle.

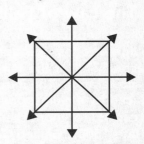

1 Make Models Fold a piece of rectangular notebook paper according to the lines of symmetry Joy drew on the rectangle. Are her lines of symmetry correct? Explain how you know.

_____

_____

2 Identify Faulty Reasoning Underline Joy's reasoning for drawing the lines of symmetry on the rectangle. What other characteristic should Joy have considered?

_____

_____

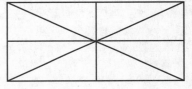

Do the Quick Lab
Using Scientific Thinking.

🔑 Assess Your Understanding

2a. Define _____ reasoning uses a general idea to make a specific observation.

b. Relate Cause and Effect What is a cause of faulty reasoning?

_____

_____

got it?

○ **I get it!** Now I know that scientific reasoning includes _____

_____

○ **I need extra help with** _____

Go to MY SCIENCE ⑤ COACH *online for help with this subject.*

Scientific Inquiry

UNLOCK THE BIG ?

🔑 **What Is Scientific Inquiry?**

🔑 **How Do You Design and Conduct an Experiment?**

🔑 **What Are Scientific Theories and Laws?**

my planeT DiARY

The Law of Falling Objects

Misconception: Heavier objects fall faster than lighter ones. This assumption is not true. They actually fall at the same rate, or with the same acceleration. The misconception was introduced by a philosopher named Aristotle and accepted for more than 2,000 years. But in the late 1500s, Galileo Galilei discovered something different—all free-falling objects fall with the same acceleration. To prove this, Galileo performed a number of experiments. Galileo's experiments involved rolling balls with different masses down a ramp called an inclined plane and making careful measurements.

Galileo and one of his acceleration experiments

MISCONCEPTION

Communicate Discuss the following questions with a partner. Write your answers below.

1. Why did Galileo perform experiments to see if all objects fall with the same acceleration?

_____

_____

2. Do you think a feather and a book that are dropped from the same height at the same time will hit the ground at the same time? Explain your answer in terms of Galileo's discovery.

_____

_____

_____

_____

_____

_____

> PLANET DIARY Go to **Planet Diary** to learn more about scientific inquiry.

 Lab zone® Do the Inquiry Warm-Up. *What's Happening?*

Vocabulary
- scientific inquiry • hypothesis • variable
- manipulated variable • responding variable
- controlled experiment • data
- scientific theory • scientific law

Skills
- ↻ Reading: Sequence
- △ Inquiry: Control Variables

What Is Scientific Inquiry?

Chirp, chirp, chirp. It is one of the hottest nights of summer and your bedroom windows are wide open. On most nights, the quiet chirping of crickets gently lulls you to sleep, but not tonight. The noise from the crickets is almost deafening. Why do all the crickets in your neighborhood seem determined to keep you awake tonight? Your thinking and questioning is the start of the **scientific inquiry** process. 🔑 **Scientific inquiry refers to the diverse ways in which scientists study the natural world and propose explanations based on the evidence they gather.** Some scientists run experiments in labs, but some cannot. For example, geologists use observations of rock layers to draw inferences about how Earth has changed over time.

Posing Questions
Scientific inquiry often begins with a question about an observation. Your observation about the frequent chirping may lead you to ask a question: Why are the crickets chirping so much tonight? Questions come from your experiences, observations, and inferences. Curiosity plays a role, too. Because others may have asked similar questions, you should do research to find what information is already known about the topic before you go on with your investigation. Look at **Figure 1** to pose a scientific question about an observation.

FIGURE 1 ···
Posing Questions
The photo at the right is of a Roesel's bush cricket from England.

 Pose Questions Make an observation about this cricket. Then pose a question about this observation that you can study.

_____

_____

_____

subheading - Red
heading = blue

Why has my digital music player stopped working?

Developing a Hypothesis How could you answer your question about cricket chirping? In trying to answer the question, you are developing a hypothesis. A **hypothesis** (plural: *hypotheses*) is a possible answer to a scientific question. You may suspect that the hot temperatures affected the chirping. Your hypothesis would be that cricket chirping increases as a result of warmer air temperatures. Use **Figure 2** to practice developing a hypothesis.

A hypothesis is *not* a fact. In science, a fact is an observation that has been confirmed repeatedly. For example, that a cricket rubs its forelegs together to make the chirping noise is a fact. A hypothesis, on the other hand, is one possible answer to a question. For example, perhaps the crickets only seemed to be chirping more that night because there were fewer other sounds than usual.

In science, a hypothesis must be testable. Researchers must be able to carry out investigations and gather evidence that will either support or disprove the hypothesis. Disproven hypotheses are still useful, because they can lead to further investigations.

FIGURE 2 ···

Developing a Hypothesis

✎ **Develop Hypotheses** Write two hypotheses that might answer this student's question.

Hypothesis A	Hypothesis B

Do the Quick Lab
Scientific Inquiry.

🔑 Assess Your Understanding

1a. Explain Can you test a hypothesis that crickets chirp more when they hide under logs? Explain.

_____

_____

_____

b. Develop Hypotheses What other hypothesis might explain why crickets chirp more frequently on some nights?

_____

_____

_____

got it? ···

○ **I get it!** Now I know that scientific inquiry is _____

_____

○ **I need extra help with** _____

Go to **MY SCIENCE** 💬 **COACH** *online for help with this subject.*

How Do You Design and Conduct an Experiment?

After developing your hypothesis, you are ready to test it by designing an experiment. ⊙— **An experiment must follow sound scientific principles for its results to be valid.** You know your experiment will involve counting cricket chirps at warm temperatures. But, how will you know how often a cricket would chirp at a low temperature? You cannot know unless you count other cricket chirps at low temperatures for comparison.

Controlling Variables To test your hypothesis, you will observe crickets at different air temperatures. All other **variables,** or factors that can change in an experiment, must be the same. This includes variables such as food and hours of daylight. By keeping these variables the same, you will know that any difference in cricket chirping is due to temperature alone.

The one variable that is purposely changed to test a hypothesis is the **manipulated variable,** or independent variable. The manipulated variable here is air temperature. The factor that may change in response to the manipulated variable is the **responding variable,** or dependent variable. The responding variable here is the number of cricket chirps.

apply it!

A student performs an experiment to determine whether 1 g of sugar or 1 g of salt dissolves more quickly in water.

1 ◢ **Control Variables** Identify the manipulated variable and the responding variable.

_____

_____

2 Identify What are two other variables in this experiment?

_____

_____

_____

3 Draw Conclusions Write a hypothesis for this experiment.

_____

_____

_____

_____

Water
Water
Water
Salt
Sugar

Setting Up a Controlled Experiment

An experiment in which only one variable is manipulated at a time is called a **controlled experiment.** You decide to test the crickets at three different temperatures: 15°C, 20°C, and 25°C, as shown in **Figure 3.** All other variables are kept the same. Otherwise, your experiment would have more than one manipulated variable. Then there would be no way to tell which variable influenced your results.

Experimental Bias

In any experiment there is a risk of introducing bias. For example, if you expect crickets to chirp more at 25°C, you may run experiments at just that temperature. Or, without meaning to, you might bias your results by selecting only the crickets that chirp the most often to test. Having a good sample size, or the number of crickets tested, is also important. Having too few crickets may bias your results because individual differences exist from cricket to cricket.

FIGURE 3 ···

A Controlled Experiment

The manipulated variable in the experiment below is temperature.

✎ **Design Experiments In the boxes, write the number of crickets you would test for this controlled experiment. On the lines below, write three other variables that must be kept the same.**

_____

_____

_____

Temperature 15°C

Crickets __83__

Temperature 20°C

Crickets __127__

Temperature 25°C

Crickets __168__

Collecting and Interpreting Data

You are almost ready to begin your experiment. You decide to test five crickets, one at a time, at each temperature. You also decide to run multiple trials for each cricket. This is because a cricket may behave differently from one trial to the next. Before you begin your experiment, decide what observations you will make and what data you will collect. **Data** are the facts, figures, and other evidence gathered through qualitative and quantitative observations. To organize your data, you may want to make a data table. A data table provides you with an organized way to collect and record your observations. Decide what your table will look like. Then you can start to collect your data.

After your data have been collected, they need to be interpreted. One tool that can help you interpret data is a graph. Graphs can reveal patterns or trends in data. Sometimes, there is more than one interpretation for a set of data. For example, scientists all agree that global temperatures have gone up over the past 100 years. What they do not agree on is how much they are likely to go up over the next 100 years.

✎

⟲ **Sequence** Underline and number the steps involved in collecting and interpreting data.

do the math!

A data table helps you organize the information you collect in an experiment. Graphing the data may reveal any patterns in your data.

❶ **Read Graphs** Identify the manipulated variable and the responding variable.

_____

_____

_____

_____

❷ **Read Graphs** As the temperature increases from 15°C to 25°C, what happens to the number of chirps per minute?

_____

_____

_____

❸ **Predict** How many chirps per minute would you expect when the temperature is 10°C?

_____

_____

Number of Chirps per Minute

Cricket	15°C	20°C	25°C
1	91	135	180
2	80	124	169
3	89	130	176
4	78	125	158
5	77	121	157
Average	83	127	168

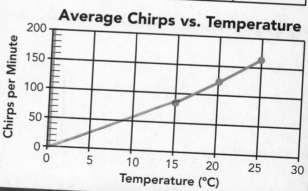

Average Chirps vs. Temperature

Chirps per Minute (y-axis: 0, 50, 100, 150, 200)

Temperature (°C) (x-axis: 0, 5, 10, 15, 20, 25, 30)

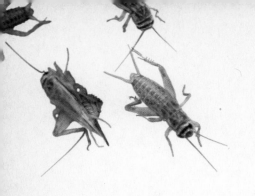

Drawing Conclusions Now you can draw conclusions about your hypothesis. A conclusion is a summary of what you have learned from an experiment. To draw your conclusion, you must examine your data objectively to see if they support or do not support your hypothesis. You also must consider whether you collected enough data.

You may decide that the data support your hypothesis. You conclude that the frequency of cricket chirping increases with temperature. Now, repeat your experiment to see if you get the same results. A conclusion is unreliable if it comes from an experiment with results that cannot be repeated. Many trials are needed before a hypothesis can be accepted as true.

Your data won't always support your hypothesis. When this happens, check your experiment for things that went wrong, or for improvements you can make. Then fix the problem and do the experiment again. If the experiment was done correctly the first time, your hypothesis was probably not correct. Propose a new hypothesis that you can test. Scientific inquiry usually doesn't end once an experiment is done. Often, one experiment leads to another.

Number of Chirps per Minute			
Cricket	15°C	20°C	25°C
1	98	100	120
2	92	95	105
3	101	93	99
4	102	85	97
5	91	89	98
Average	96	92	103

FIGURE 4 ···

▷VIRTUAL LAB Drawing Conclusions
Sometimes the same experiment can have very different data.

✎ **Answer the questions below.**

1. **Interpret Tables** Look at the data in the table. Do the data support the hypothesis that crickets chirp more in warmer temperatures? Explain.

_____

_____

_____

2. **Analyze Sources of Error** If the data in this table were yours, what might you do next? Explain.

_____

_____

_____

3. **CHALLENGE** Can you draw a conclusion from these data? Why or why not?

_____

_____

_____

Communicating Communicating is the sharing of ideas and results with others through writing and speaking. Scientists communicate by giving talks at scientific meetings, exchanging information on the Internet, or publishing articles in scientific journals.

When scientists share the results of their research, they describe their procedures so that others can repeat their experiments. It is important for scientists to wait until an experiment has been repeated many times before accepting a result. Therefore, scientists must keep accurate records of their methods and results. This way, scientists know that the result is accurate. Before the results are published, other scientists review the experiment for sources of error, such as bias, data interpretation, and faulty conclusions.

Sometimes, a scientific inquiry can be part of a huge project in which many scientists are working together around the world. For example, the Human Genome Project involved scientists from 18 different countries. The scientists' goal was to create a map of the information in your cells that makes you who you are. On such a large project, scientists must share their ideas and results regularly. Come up with ideas for communicating the results of your cricket experiment in **Figure 5.**

Vocabulary Identify Related Word Forms *Communication* is the noun form of the verb *communicate*. Write a sentence using the noun *communication*.

_____

_____

_____

_____

The Human Genome Project logo

FIGURE 5 ······································
Communicating Results
Since the Human Genome Project touched upon many areas of science, communication was important.

✎ **Communicate** **Get together as a group and write three ways to share the results of your cricket experiment with other students.**

Biology-

Physics-

Ethics-

Chemistry-

Informatics

In a Scientist's Shoes

EXPLORE THE BIG ?

How do scientists investigate the natural world?

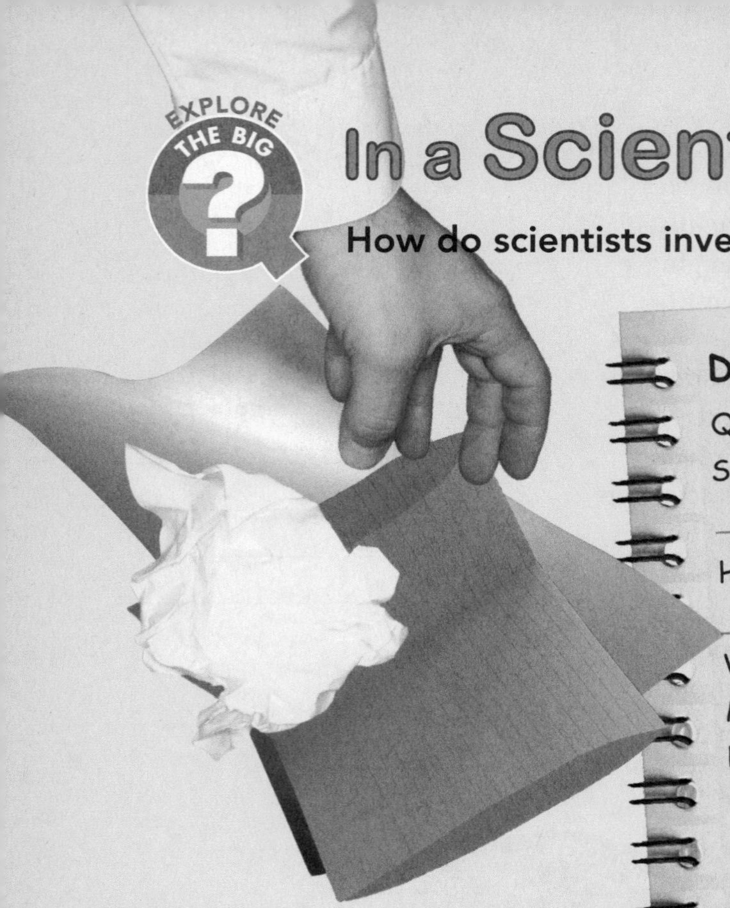

Design an Experiment

QUESTION _____

SCIENTIFIC ATTITUDES INVOLVED _____

_____

HYPOTHESIS _____

VARIABLES

Manipulated Variables _____

Responding Variables _____

Factors to Consider _____

_____

COLLECT DATA

Number of Trials _____

Units of Measure _____

SCIENTIFIC SKILLS USED _____

_____

NEXT STEPS _____

_____

FIGURE 6 ·······································

> INTERACTIVE ART When you think like a scientist, you develop hypotheses and design experiments to test them.

✎ **Design Experiments** Think like a scientist to find out which falls fastest: an unfolded sheet of paper, a sheet of paper folded in fourths, or a crumpled sheet of paper.

Lab zone® Do the Lab Investigation *Keeping Flowers Fresh.*

⚷ Assess Your Understanding

2a. Name Name two ways scientists communicate their results.

_____

_____

_____

_____

b. ANSWER THE BIG ? How do scientists investigate the natural world?

_____

_____

_____

_____

got it? ··

○ **I get it!** Now I know that an experimental design must _____

_____

○ **I need extra help with** _____

Go to MY SCIENCE ⓢ COACH online for help with this subject.

What Are Scientific Theories and Laws?

Sometimes, a large set of related observations can be connected by a single explanation. This explanation can lead to the development of a scientific theory. In everyday life, a theory can be an unsupported guess. Everyday theories are not scientific theories. A **scientific theory** is a well-tested explanation for a wide range of observations and experimental results. For example, according to the atomic theory, all substances are composed of particles called atoms. Atomic theory helps to explain many observations, such as why iron nails rust. Scientists accept a theory only when it can explain the important observations. If the theory cannot explain new observations, then the theory is changed or thrown out. In this way, theories are constantly being developed, revised, or discarded as more information is collected.

A **scientific law** is a statement that describes what scientists expect to happen every time under a particular set of conditions. 🔑 **Unlike a theory, a scientific law describes an observed pattern in nature without attempting to explain it.** For example, the law of gravity states that all objects in the universe attract each other. Look at **Figure 7.**

FIGURE 7 ·································
A Scientific Law
According to the law of gravity, this parachutist will eventually land on Earth.

✏️ **Apply Concepts** Give another example of a scientific law.

_____

_____

_____

Lab zone® Do the Quick Lab
Theories and Laws.

🔑 Assess Your Understanding

got it? ···

○ **I get it!** Now I know that the difference between a scientific theory and a law is that _____

_____

○ **I need extra help with** _____

    Go to **my science s coach** online for help with this subject.

1 Study Guide

To think like a scientist, you must use _____, _____,
and _____ to observe the world.

LESSON 1 Science and the Natural World

🔑 Scientists use skills such as observing, inferring, predicting, classifying, evaluating, and making models to study the world.

Vocabulary
- science • observing
- quantitative observation
- qualitative observation • inferring
- predicting • classifying • evaluating
- making models

LESSON 2 Thinking Like a Scientist

🔑 Scientists possess certain important attitudes, including curiosity, honesty, creativity, open-mindedness, skepticism, good ethics, and awareness of bias.

🔑 Scientific reasoning requires a logical way of thinking based on gathering and evaluating evidence.

Vocabulary
- skepticism • ethics • personal bias • cultural bias
- experimental bias • objective • subjective
- deductive reasoning • inductive reasoning

LESSON 3 Scientific Inquiry

🔑 Scientific inquiry refers to the diverse ways in which scientists study the natural world and propose explanations based on the evidence they gather.

🔑 An experiment must follow sound scientific principles for its results to be valid.

🔑 Unlike a theory, a scientific law describes an observed pattern in nature without attempting to explain it.

Vocabulary
- scientific inquiry • hypothesis • variable • manipulated variable • responding variable
- controlled experiment • data • scientific theory • scientific law

Review and Assessment

LESSON 1 Science and the Natural World

1. When you explain or interpret an observation, you are

  a. making models.   **b.** classifying.

  c. inferring.   (**d.**) predicting.

2. When scientists group observations that are alike in some way, they are _____

3. Predict How do scientists use observations to make predictions?

_____

_____

_____

4. Infer Suppose you come home to the scene below. What can you infer happened?

There are 2 fishes. ✓

The fish are on the right r side. ✓ (*tank*)

5. Observe What is a quantitative observation you might make in your school cafeteria?

The fish are having this eight-side because they are finding an other onx the other side

LESSON 2 Thinking Like a Scientist

6. The scientific attitude of having doubt is called

  a. open-mindedness.   **b.** curiosity.

  c. honesty.   **d.** skepticism.

7. When a person allows personal opinions, values, or tastes to influence a conclusion, that person is using _____ reasoning.

8. Compare and Contrast Describe the three types of bias that can influence a science experiment.

_____

_____

_____

_____

_____

_____

_____

9. Draw Conclusions Why is it important to report experimental results honestly, even when the results might be the opposite of the results you expect to see?

_____

_____

_____

_____

_____

10. Write About It A team of scientists is developing a new medicine to improve memory. Write about how the attitudes of curiosity, honesty, creativity, and open-mindedness help the scientists in their work. When might they need to think about ethics? How could bias influence their results?

29

LESSON 3 Scientific Inquiry

11. The facts, figures, and other evidence gathered through observations are called
    - a. conclusions.
    - b. data.
    - c. predictions.
    - d. hypotheses.

12. The one variable that is changed to test a hypothesis is
    - a. the responding variable.
    - b. the other variable.
    - c. the manipulated variable.
    - d. the dependent variable.

13. A _____ is a well-tested explanation for a wide range of observations.

14. **Communicate** What are some ways that scientists communicate with each other?

    _____
    _____
    _____
    _____
    _____
    _____
    _____

15. 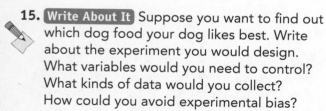 **Write About It** Suppose you want to find out which dog food your dog likes best. Write about the experiment you would design. What variables would you need to control? What kinds of data would you collect? How could you avoid experimental bias?

 APPLY THE BIG ?

How do scientists investigate the natural world?

16. Central Middle School is having problems with attendance during the winter. Many students get sick and miss school. The principal wants to fix the problem, but she is not sure what to do. One idea is to install hand sanitizer dispensers in the classrooms.

Think about this problem scientifically. What is a possible hypothesis in this situation? What experiment could you design to test it? Mention at least three attitudes or skills that will be important in finding the answer.

Hypothesi is an
educated guess. I
guess that they
would have hand
Sanitizer ☺

_____
_____
_____
_____
_____
_____
_____
_____
_____

Standardized Test Prep

Multiple Choice

Circle the letter of the best answer.

1. Sophia noticed that many birds pick through the seeds in her bird feeder until they get a sunflower seed. What is an inference she could make from this observation?

   A Birds are attracted to white objects.

   B Sunflower seeds are crunchy.

   C Birds do not like seeds.

   D Birds prefer sunflower seeds.

2. Which of the following attitudes do good scientists possess?

   A curiosity about the world

   B certainty that a hypothesis is correct

   C ambition to be famous and respected

   D a strong sense of cultural bias

3. Marie observed people at a store. Which is a qualitative observation she may have made?

   A Twenty people walked into the store.

   B The store sells clothes.

   C It was 1:00 P.M.

   D all of the above

4. Which of the following statements best describes a scientific theory?

   A It is a well-tested explanation for a wide range of experimental results.

   B It is an educated guess based on experience.

   C It is a statement that describes what scientists expect to happen.

   D It is a hypothesis that was confirmed by an experiment.

5. Tara was collecting data about rainfall by measuring water levels in a bucket in her yard. She saw her dog drinking from the bucket. This is an example of

   A cultural bias.

   B personal bias.

   C experimental bias.

   D data collection.

Constructed Response

Use the graph below and your knowledge of science to help you answer Question 6. Write your answer on a separate sheet of paper.

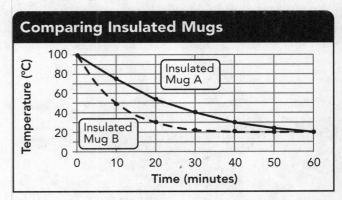

6. This graph compares how well two different brands of insulated mugs retain heat. Describe the variables in the experiment. What conclusion might you draw from the graph?

When We Think We Know
but It Isn't So

Science is a way of thinking and learning about the world. It is not rigid or unchanging. In fact, scientists are constantly learning new things. And sometimes, they make mistakes! That's just what René Blondlot and his co-workers at Nancy University in France did in 1903.

X-rays had just been discovered. Scientists everywhere, including Blondlot, were experimenting with them. In a series of photographs taken in an experiment, Blondlot observed strange lights. He was convinced he had discovered another new form of radiation. He named his discovery the N-ray, in honor of Nancy University where he worked. Dozens of other scientists repeated his experiments expecting to see the lights. Some were convinced that they actually had seen them. But there was one very big problem—N-rays do not exist! Scientists who were skeptical did not see these lights and could not repeat the results of the experiment. It was soon discovered that when they looked for N-rays, Blondlot and his colleagues were just seeing what they expected and hoped to see.

This is a clear case of expectations influencing observations. Because some scientists did not do enough to avoid their bias, they made a big mistake.

Research It Research about Robert W. Wood, the scientist who disproved the existence of N-rays. Write a paragraph summarizing how he came to this conclusion. What questions did he ask?

◄ René Blondlot was a famous scientist who allowed his ambition to overrule his powers of observation.

READY FOR A CLOSE-UP

Whether they are filming animal behavior in the wild or documenting new medical technologies, science filmmakers never know what's going to happen next. For one film, a filmmaker spent 16 weeks sitting hidden under an animal skin for 14 hours every day, just so he could film bird behavior. To film a lion attack, another film crew put themselves in danger by parking a few meters away from some very hungry lions in the middle of the night.

Making a good science film is about more than getting the perfect shot. Crews working in fragile ecosystems like the Arctic or in deserts take care not to wreck habitats. This means they travel light—sometimes using just one hand-held camera.

Writers and producers also try to avoid bias. If there is more than one theory about a topic, they try to find experts who can discuss each theory, and they present as many facts as possible. The makers of a film about the Jarkov woolly mammoth relied heavily on their scientific advisors to make sure scientific facts weren't sacrificed for a good story.

Patience, an adventurous spirit, and science knowledge are all part of being a great science filmmaker!

Research It Research one species of animal. Write a proposal for a documentary about that animal. Include a list of four or five questions you hope to answer with your film.

WHY HAVE COMPUTERS CHANGED?

THE BIG ?

How do science and society affect each other?

Technology has changed. A 1950s computer that used to fill an entire room can now be held in your hands. The telephone that used to be attached by a cord in order to work is now not only portable, but can also play music, take photos, and search the Internet. Television is now larger, digital, and in high definition.

⚠ **Infer Why do you think technology, like computers, phones, and television, has changed over time?**

_____

_____

_____

_____

> UNTAMED SCIENCE Watch the **Untamed Science** video to learn more about how science and society interact.

Science, Society, and You

2 Getting Started

Check Your Understanding

1. **Background** Read the paragraph below and then answer the question.

> Should Nina's family buy a hybrid car or a conventional car? Conventional cars run on gasoline, a limited **resource**. Hybrid cars use a combination of gasoline and electricity. To help her family make a decision, Nina looks at the **research** on hybrid cars and evaluates the **reliability** of the data on Web sites.

A material or living thing that people can use is a **resource.**

Research is a careful study of a subject to discover new facts or test new ideas.

Reliability is the extent to which data can be trusted to be accurate or correct.

- Why is it important for Nina to research hybrid cars and evaluate the reliability of data on Web sites?

_____

_____

_____

▷ **MY READING WEB** If you had trouble completing the question above, visit **My Reading Web** and type in *Science, Society, and You.*

Vocabulary Skill

Use Context to Determine Meaning Science texts often contain unknown words. Look for context clues in surrounding words and phrases to figure out the meaning of a new word. In the paragraph below, look for clues to the meaning of *controversial.*

Sometimes a scientist's work is in conflict with the beliefs of society. As a result, the work is *controversial.* A controversy is a public disagreement between groups with different views. For instance, Galileo's model of Earth revolving around the sun was *controversial* because it conflicted with society's beliefs in the 1600s.

2. **Quick Check** In the paragraph above, circle the phrase that helps you understand the meaning of the word *controversial.*

Introduction to Vocabulary	a scientist's work is in conflict with the beliefs of society
Word	controversial, *adj.*
Definition	of, subject to, or stirring up controversy
Example	Galileo's model of Earth revolving around the sun

benefit

opinion

life science

earth and space science

Chapter Preview

LESSON 1
- cost
- benefit
- ↻ Compare and Contrast
- △ Pose Questions

LESSON 2
- scientific literacy
- evidence
- opinion
- ↻ Summarize
- △ Interpret Data

LESSON 3
- controversy
- ↻ Sequence
- △ Predict

LESSON 4
- life science
- earth and space science
- physical science
- ↻ Identify the Main Idea
- △ Communicate

> VOCAB FLASH CARDS For extra help with vocabulary, visit **Vocab Flash Cards** and type in *Science, Society, and You.*

UNLOCK THE BIG ?

🔑 **Why Is Science Important?**

my planeT DiaRY

Recycled Homes

Have you ever wondered what happens to the materials that people recycle? In 1990, a builder decided to use some of these materials to build his house in Montana. Completed in 1992, the house is constructed almost entirely of recycled materials. Some of these materials are fluorescent bulb casings, car windshield glass, wood chips that would usually be discarded, sawdust, and plastic milk jugs. The builder designed the house to look similar to other houses. He wanted to show people that it is possible to construct houses made of recycled materials without sacrificing the style that people are used to seeing. Many houses built today might include recycled materials.

Communicate Discuss the following question with a partner. Then write your answer below.

What other products or structures do you think could be built with recycled materials?

_____

_____

_____

▶ PLANET DIARY Go to **Planet Diary** to learn more about science.

Lab zone® Do the Inquiry Warm-Up *How Much Do You See or Hear About Science?*

Vocabulary	Skills
• cost • benefit	Reading: Compare and Contrast Inquiry: Pose Questions

Why Is Science Important?

Where is it safe to be during a thunderstorm? Can you catch a cold from getting wet on a rainy day? The answers to questions like these are based on science. **Understanding scientific principles and thinking scientifically can help you solve problems and answer questions throughout your life.**

Becoming an Informed Consumer If you have ever bought something in a store, you are a consumer. To become an informed consumer, you need to know if the products you buy are safe. For example, you might want to know why some foods are recalled from grocery stores. Science can help you understand the reasons for a recall and help you protect yourself in the future.

As a consumer you may also want to know how things work. Studying science can help you understand how products work, including the helmets and bikes you see in **Figure 1.** Understanding how things work will help you make better choices about the products you buy and use.

did you
know? ....

Did you know that government agencies can help you become an informed consumer? The Food and Drug Administration and the Federal Trade Commission, help make sure that you know everything about food and other products before you buy them.

FIGURE 1 ···

Science in Everyday Life

Learning science can make activities such as biking safer and more fun for you.

✎ **Pose Questions Write in the chart two questions that you can research about safe biking. Then do the same for how a bike works.**

Safe biking	
How a bike works	

39

Compare and Contrast

How are a cost and a benefit alike? How are they different?

_____
_____
_____
_____
_____
_____

Experimental cars run on fuels other than gasoline.

_____
_____
_____
_____
_____

Becoming an Informed Citizen Should water use be limited? Should astronauts explore space? People must make informed decisions about such issues. Before making an informed decision, you need to know the costs and benefits of taking an action. A **cost** is a negative result of either taking or not taking action. A **benefit** is a positive consequence of either taking or not taking an action. Knowing science helps you identify and analyze costs and benefits and make informed decisions about an issue. Try identifying the costs and benefits of the products shown in **Figure 2**.

FIGURE 2 ....

Product Costs and Benefits

In evaluating a product's costs and benefits, different people may make different decisions.

✎ **Analyze Costs and Benefits** Write a cost or a benefit of having each of the products shown below.

Some sweatshirts are made of polyester fleece, which is made from recycled plastic bottles instead of cotton.

_____
_____
_____
_____

Personal Digital Assistants and cell phones are common electronic devices.

_____
_____
_____
_____

apply it!

Earth's resources are limited. The wise use of these resources affects many parts of your everyday life. You may have thought about the following issue. Should you put your lunch in a plastic bag or a reusable bag?

1 **Evaluate the Impact on Society** Working in a small group, identify a cost and benefit for each type of bag. Then circle the bag you decide to carry.

Type of Bag	Cost	Benefit
Plastic bag		
Reusable bag		

2 **Pose Questions** How would you find more information about the costs and benefits of each bag? What questions would you ask?

_____

_____

_____

Lab zone® Do the Quick Lab *Using Science.*

🔑 Assess Your Understanding

1a. Define What is a benefit?

_____

_____

_____

b. CHALLENGE What can help you make an informed decision?

_____

_____

_____

got it? ....

○ **I get it!** Now I know that understanding scientific principles and thinking scientifically can _____

_____

○ I need extra help with _____

Go to MY SCIENCE 🔘 COACH *online for help with this subject.*

Scientific Literacy

UNLOCK THE BIG ?

🔑 **Why Is Scientific Literacy Important?**

🔑 **How Do You Analyze Scientific Claims?**

🔑 **How Do You Research Scientific Questions?**

my planeT DiaRY

Why Do You Need to Know?

If you watch TV crime programs, then you know that investigators often use DNA testing to solve a case. How does DNA testing help? Scientists can identify people by examining their DNA. A person's DNA is unique, like a person's fingerprint.

In the future, you may need more information about DNA evidence than what is given in TV programs. For example, if you are selected to sit on a jury in a trial that uses DNA evidence, you will want to know scientific details about DNA to make your decision.

FUN FACTS

Communicate Discuss the question with a partner. Then write your answer below.

A DNA sample links an accused suspect to a crime. Suppose there is a one in ten million chance that the DNA sample comes from someone else. How would this affect your decision as a juror?

_____

_____

_____

_____

_____

> PLANET DIARY Go to **Planet Diary** to learn more about scientific literacy.

Lab zone® Do the Inquiry Warm-Up *Posing Questions.*

Why Is Scientific Literacy Important?

Suppose someone asks you to sign a petition to protect the Canada geese in your town. "People are trying to keep the geese away from our parks!" he says. A person standing nearby says, "But the geese make an awful mess." You're confused. You know you need to learn more about the issue.

Vocabulary
• scientific literacy   • evidence
• opinion

Skills
↻ Reading: Summarize
△ Inquiry: Interpret Data

Scientific Literacy   To understand the many issues you encounter, you need scientific literacy. **Scientific literacy** means understanding scientific terms and principles well enough to ask questions, evaluate information, and make decisions. ⚷ **By having scientific literacy, you will be able to identify good sources of scientific information, evaluate them for accuracy, and apply the knowledge to questions or problems in your life.**

Evidence and Opinion   To evaluate scientific information, you must first distinguish between evidence and opinion. In science, **evidence** includes observations and conclusions that have been repeated. Evidence may or may not support a scientific claim. An **opinion** is an idea that may be formed from evidence but has not been confirmed by evidence. In **Figure 1,** try separating evidence from opinion.

↻ **Summarize** In your own words, summarize the second paragraph.

_____
_____
_____
_____
_____
_____
_____
_____

FIGURE 1 ···
Evidence and Opinion
Should your town try to keep Canada geese away from the parks?

✎ **Distinguish Evidence and Opinion** Under each statement in the boxes, label the statement as evidence or opinion.

Geese spend up to 12 hours a day eating grass and roots.
Evidence

Geese are too messy.
Opinion

Lab zone ® Do the Quick Lab
Scientific Literacy Survey.

⚷ Assess Your Understanding

got it? ···

O **I get it!** Now I know that by having scientific literacy _____

_____

O **I need extra help with** _____

   Go to my science ⊙ coach *online for help with this subject.*

How Do You Analyze Scientific Claims?

Scientific literacy gives you the tools to analyze scientific claims. Scientific reasoning gives you the process. 🔑 **You can use scientific reasoning to analyze scientific claims by looking for bias and errors in the research, evaluating data, and identifying faulty reasoning.**

FIGURE 2 ···

Analyzing Scientific Claims

✎ **Read about this research and think about the researcher's conclusion. Then answer the question in each box.**

A researcher needs to find out if people in a town have good computer skills. The researcher advertises online for participants to take the test. He offers a free thumb drive as a payment.

Twenty people take the test. Everyone gets a perfect score.

The researcher concludes that the town's residents have excellent computer skills.

Identify Experimental Bias What is an important source of experimental bias in this research?

_____

_____

_____

Analyze Sources of Error What is an important source of error in this research?

_____

_____

_____

_____

apply it!

Read the sample advertisement. Then use scientific reasoning to analyze its claims.

1 Interpret Data How many subjects were in the study?

_____

2 Evaluate Scientific Claims Do the research results support the claim that using *KnowHow* helps people get better grades? Explain your answer.

_____
_____
_____
_____

3 CHALLENGE Was Subject B's score actually 25% higher than Subject A's score? Calculate.

_____
_____

Improve Your Test Scores!

A scientifically proven new way to get better grades!

Just look at our research results.

Subject A: Studied for 30 minutes in front of the TV and didn't use our product. Scored 72 points!

Subject B: Studied for 3 hours with a tutor and used KnowHow! Scored 90 points!

That means **25% HIGHER GRADES** with **KnowHow!**

You CAN make the grade! ORDER **KnowHow** TODAY!

Lab zone® Do the Quick Lab Analyzing Claims.

🔑 **Assess Your Understanding**

1a. Identify What is one way to use scientific reasoning to analyze scientific claims?

_____
_____

b. Make Generalizations Would a scientific claim based on one test be a good claim? Why or why not?

_____
_____
_____

got it?

○ **I get it!** Now I know that I can analyze scientific claims by _____

_____
_____

○ **I need extra help with** _____

Go to **MY SCIENCE** Ⓢ **COACH** online for help with this subject.

How Do You Research Scientific Questions?

Chances are you will need to answer scientific questions to make decisions in your life. For example, suppose you injure your knee and the doctor gives you a choice of treatments. You need to do research before deciding. In science, you also need to do research to design an experiment.

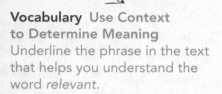 **To make decisions and design experiments, you need relevant and reliable background information.** Relevant information is knowledge that relates to the question. Reliable information comes from a person or organization that is not biased. Generally, universities, museums, and government agencies are sources of reliable information. So are many nonfiction books, magazines, and educational Web sites. Look at the sources in **Figure 3**.

Vocabulary Use Context to Determine Meaning Underline the phrase in the text that helps you understand the word *relevant*.

FIGURE 3 ·····································

Evaluating Sources of Information

✎ **Evaluate Data Reliability** Circle the most relevant and reliable source of information for your research about water use in your community. Explain your choice below.

_____

_____

_____

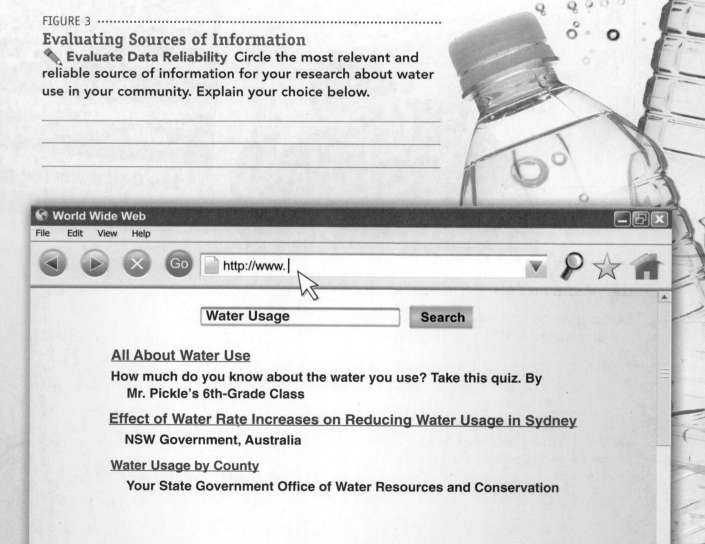

World Wide Web

File   Edit   View   Help

http://www.

Water Usage   Search

All About Water Use
How much do you know about the water you use? Take this quiz. By Mr. Pickle's 6th-Grade Class

Effect of Water Rate Increases on Reducing Water Usage in Sydney
NSW Government, Australia

Water Usage by County
Your State Government Office of Water Resources and Conservation

EXPLORE THE BIG ? All Bottled Up!

How do science and society affect each other?

1 Clear plastics that could be used to make light, cheap bottles were invented.

2 Manufacturers made many plastic bottles for many beverages, which people buy.

3 Empty plastic bottles became litter. Bottle deposit laws encouraged recycling empty bottles.

4 Ways to recycle bottles into new, safe products were invented.

5 People bought products made from recycled bottles.

6 Bottles that use 30% less plastic were designed.

FIGURE 4 ....
▸ REAL-WORLD INQUIRY Science and society are interconnected.

✎ Infer Circle the boxes that show the work of science. Then explain below how the statements in boxes 3 and 4 show how science and other aspects of society affect each other.

_____
_____
_____
_____

 Lab zone® Do the Quick Lab Sources of Information.

🔑 Assess Your Understanding

2a. Review What is information that relates to a question called?

_____

b. ANSWER THE BIG ? How do science and society affect each other?

_____
_____
_____
_____
_____

got it? ....

○ I get it! Now I know that to make informed decisions and design experiments, you need _____

_____

○ I need extra help with _____

Go to MY SCIENCE ⓢ COACH online for help with this subject.

47

🔑 **How Does Society Affect the Work of Scientists?**

UNLOCK THE BIG **?**

MY PLANET DIARY

VOICES FROM HISTORY

Albert Einstein

Born in 1879 in Germany, Albert Einstein is recognized as one of history's most brilliant scientists. He is best known for his physics equation $E = mc^2$, which describes his theory of relativity. E stands for energy, m stands for mass, and c stands for the speed of light. This equation describes the relationship between mass and energy. Here are two of Einstein's quotations.

"No amount of experimentation can ever prove me right; a single experiment can prove me wrong."

"Intellectual growth should commence at birth and cease only at death."

Read the following question. Write your answer below.

What do you think Einstein was saying about science in the first quotation?

Never ever stop what you are doing it will come true

> PLANET DIARY Go to **Planet Diary** to learn more about scientists and society.

Lab zone® Do the Inquiry Warm-Up *What Do Scientists Do?*

$$f(x,y,z) = \frac{}{\partial x} + \frac{}{\partial y} + \frac{}{\partial z}$$

$$E = mc^2$$

$$y = \int f(x)dx$$

Vocabulary
• controversy

Skills
↻ Reading: Sequence
△ Inquiry: Predict

How Does Society Affect the Work of Scientists?

Science discoveries have helped to bring cars, computers, phones, and other products to society. And today's scientists are working on tomorrow's discoveries. ⚷ **The work that scientists do changes society. In turn, society influences the work of scientists.**

Sometimes scientific work conflicts with the beliefs of a society or its leaders. When this happens, a scientist's work can cause a **controversy,** or a public disagreement between groups. Scientific controversies are not uncommon. By defending their work, scientists have helped people better understand the world.

Galileo Galilei For many years, Galileo Galilei observed the night sky with a telescope. In 1610, he published his discoveries supporting the heliocentric model, a model of the universe in which Earth moves around the sun. This heliocentric model, shown at the right, conflicted with the beliefs of his society's leaders. In 1616, all books that supported this model were banned. In 1632, Galileo published another book that supported this model. As a result, he was tried, found guilty, and lived the rest of his life under house arrest. In time though, Galileo's work led to an acceptance of science as a way of explaining the natural world.

Galileo's diagram of the heliocentric model

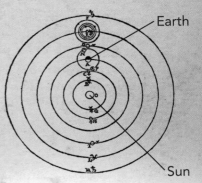

Earth

Sun

↻ **Sequence** Write in your own words the order of events that led to Galileo's house arrest.

Event 1	Event 2	Event 3

Event 4	Event 5	Event 6
		Galileo was placed under house arrest.

Ignaz Semmelweis

Ignaz Semmelweis was a young doctor working in a hospital in Austria in the 1840s. He observed that many women died of infections after giving birth in the hospital. After studying the problem, he suggested that doctors wash their hands before delivering babies. As soon as doctors started doing this, death rates dropped. However, Semmelweis's solution to the problem was in conflict with common medical practices at the time. Therefore, Semmelweis lost his job at the hospital. Eventually, new discoveries about disease supported Semmelweis's ideas. Hand-washing before deliveries became routine, and many more mothers survived.

Rachel Carson

Rachel Carson was a biologist who wrote about science and nature. Her last book, *Silent Spring*, was published in 1962. This book is about the effects of pesticides, such as DDT, on the environment. Pesticides are chemicals that farmers can use to kill insects that harm their crops. After World War II, farmers used pesticides and their harvests increased. However, large numbers of birds and other animals died as a result of pesticide use. Carson used data to show how pesticides harmed animals, but many people disagreed with her ideas. Yet, in 1972, the government banned DDT, and *Silent Spring* played an important role in the government's decision. Eventually, most wildlife populations recovered from the harm DDT caused.

FIGURE 1 ....

> **INTERACTIVE ART** **Effects of DDT**

High concentrations of DDT in the environment caused birds to lay eggs with thin, fragile shells that would break easily.

✎ **Communicate** Discuss with a partner why you think people were resistant to the ideas of Semmelweis and Carson despite being presented with data that prove their points. Then write your answer below.

_____

_____

_____

_____

_____

_____

apply it!

Suppose that fish in your town's river are dying. Scientists conclude that polluted water from a nearby factory is killing the fish. If it costs too much to fix the problem, the factory will have to close. Many people in town work in the factory. Many others work in fishing camps that attract tourists who come for the great fishing.

1 **Predict** Do you think each group below will reject or agree with the conclusion about why the fish are dying? Explain each answer.

Factory workers

_____

_____

Fishing camp owners

_____

_____

_____

2 **CHALLENGE** What would be a cost and a benefit if the town offered to fix the problem for the factory?

_____

_____

_____

 **Do the Quick Lab** *Light Sources.*

🔑 Assess Your Understanding

1a. Define What is a scientific controversy?

_____

_____

_____

b. Explain Why was there controversy over Semmelweis's ideas?

_____

_____

_____

_____

got it? ....

○ **I get it!** Now I know that science and society affect each other because _____

_____

○ **I need extra help with** _____

Go to **MY SCIENCE** ⓢ **COACH** online for help with this subject.

UNLOCK
THE BIG
?

🔑 **What Are Some Science Careers?**

🔑 **Why Do Scientists Work Together?**

🔑 **How Is Science Important in Non-Science Careers?**

my planeT DiaRY

CAREER

Robotics Scientist

Have you ever seen a movie in which robots talk like people, show emotions, think, and basically act almost human? Although these robots don't commonly exist today, they may in the future, thanks to robotics scientists.

One such scientist is Maja Matarić. Her research is aimed at designing the behaviors of robots so they can help people in different ways. This research enables Matarić not only to work with computer science, but also to explore other branches of science. How does working with robots every day sound to you?

Read the following question. Then write your answer below.

Why do you think Dr. Matarić must consider multiple areas of science when doing her research?

_____

_____

_____

_____

_____

▶ PLANET DIARY Go to **Planet Diary** to learn more about careers in science.

Lab **zone** Do the Inquiry Warm-Up *What Do Scientists Look Like?*

What Are Some Science Careers?

You know about some science careers, such as those of astronauts and doctors. But do you know about volcanologists, who study volcanoes, and ornithologists, who study birds? Scientists work in three major areas. 🔑 **The three main areas of science careers are life science, earth and space science, and physical science.**

Vocabulary
- life science
- earth and space science
- physical science

Skills
- ↪ Reading: Identify the Main Idea
- ⚠ Inquiry: Communicate

Life Science

Life science is the study of living things, including plants, animals, and microscopic life forms. Life scientists also study how living things interact with each other and with their surroundings. The study of the human body is part of life sciences, too. **Figure 1** shows just a few examples of life science careers.

FIGURE 1 ···

Life Science Careers

✎ **Infer** Read about each career and then identify the kinds of problems each scientist might solve.

Life Sciences Career	Problems Scientists Might Solve
Biomedical Researchers	
Entomologists	
Fisheries Scientists	

Biomedical Researchers find new treatments for diseases and ways to improve existing treatments. They work for hospitals, drug companies, and the government.

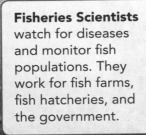

Fisheries Scientists watch for diseases and monitor fish populations. They work for fish farms, fish hatcheries, and the government.

Entomologists study insects and their roles in the environment. They work for food companies, universities, and the government.

53

Identify the Main Idea
Underline the main idea in the paragraph. Then circle details that support the main idea.

Earth and Space Science Earth scientists study areas of **earth and space science,** which is the study of Earth and its place in the universe. Some earth scientists study the forces that have shaped Earth throughout its history. Others study Earth's oceans, its fresh water, or its weather. Space scientists study the planets and stars that exist beyond Earth. **Figure 2** shows a few examples of earth and space science careers.

FIGURE 2 ·······································

Careers in Earth and Space Science and Physical Science

✎ **Answer the following questions.**

1. **Ask Questions** What question would you like to ask an earth and space scientist?

_____

_____

2. **Explain** Which physical science career sounds the most interesting? Why?

_____

_____

_____

Astrophysicists research the universe beyond Earth. They use instruments to detect light and other radiation from stars and other objects. Most astrophysicists do research and teach at universities.

Hydrologists investigate fresh water and its movement. They give advice on how new construction might affect water movement. They plan projects to reduce flood damage. Hydrologists might work for environmental consulting firms, construction companies, and the government.

Geoscientists study Earth. Some focus on movements in the crust that cause earthquakes. Others study rocks, minerals, or resources such as petroleum. Geoscientists may work for oil companies, civil engineering firms, universities, and the government.

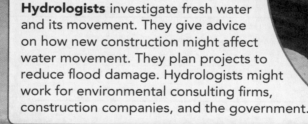

Physical Science

Physical science includes the study of energy, motion, sound, light, electricity, and magnetism. It also includes chemistry—the study of the matter that makes up all things. Below are a few examples of physical science careers.

Chemists have a wide range of jobs. They research the nature of matter and develop new materials. They work for research labs, food and drug companies, and many other employers.

Physical Science Technicians set up experiments, run tests, and maintain equipment for scientists. They solve problems as they arise. Technicians work for manufacturers, research labs, power plants, and the government.

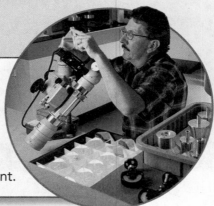

Physics Teachers educate students about physics. They evaluate students' learning in lab and classroom settings. Physics teachers work for high schools, colleges, and universities.

Newton's gravitational law.

$F = \dfrac{g \times m_1 m_2}{}$

$g = 1.01$
$g = $ constant

$m_1 = m_1$
$m_2 = m_2$
$d = $

$m_1 (block) = 5.57 \text{ g}$
$m_2 (table) = 150.2 \text{ g}$
$d = 10 \text{ meters}$

$F = (1.01)(5.57)(150.2)$

---

do the
math!

This table shows the percentage of scientists working for various categories of U.S. employers.

Where Scientists Work	
For-Profit Business and Industry	59%
Nonprofit Organizations	6%
Education (K–12)	7%
Self-Employed	6%
Government	13%
Colleges and Universities	9%

❶ Calculate What percentage of scientists work either for the government or for a nonprofit organization?

_____

❷ Interpret Data In which category do fewer scientists work compared to business and industry?

⭕ government
⭕ education
⭕ nonprofit organizations
⭕ all of the above

Lab zone® Do the Quick Lab *Branches of Science*.

🔑 Assess Your Understanding

got it?

⭕ **I get it!** Now I know that the three main areas of science careers are _____

_____

_____

⭕ **I need extra help with** _____

Go to **MY SCIENCE ⓢ COACH** *online for help with this subject.*

Why Do Scientists Work Together?

Think about working on a puzzle with friends. You probably all work on different sections at the same time. Scientists work in a similar way. 🔑 Most scientists work in teams with scientists from other fields. This is because most scientific questions need the work of scientists from many fields to answer them. Look at Figure 3 and Figure 4 to see how scientists work together to reach goals.

FIGURE 3 ···

Exploring Space

Astronauts live on the International Space Station, which orbits about 400 kilometers above Earth. Scientists from many fields work to address the challenges of living in space.

✏️ **Complete these tasks.**

Food Scientists develop special food for space travel. They make healthful and tasty food that is packaged securely and is easy to prepare.
✏️ **Infer** Identify other scientists that provide food for astronauts. Then describe what they do.

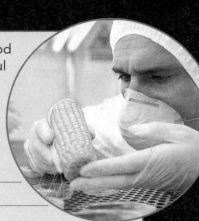

_____

_____

_____

_____

_____

Astronauts on the space station study such things as how living in space affects muscle strength, and whether or not crops can be grown in space.
✏️ **Classify** Explain which area of science is involved in these experiments and why.

_____

_____

_____

Materials Scientists study the properties of materials such as ceramics to understand how they would perform in space.
✏️ **Identify** Name some other projects that materials scientists might work on.

_____

_____

FIGURE 4 ··································
Developing Biofuels
Scientists from many fields work together
to develop biofuels made from soybeans
or other plant matter.

✎ Pose Questions For each scientist, write
a question that they might investigate to
reach the goal of developing biofuels.

Botanists study plants—
where they grow and
what they need to
grow. Question:

_____
_____
_____
_____

Soil Scientists study soil, identify the minerals
and nutrients it contains, and figure out how
to use crops to improve the soil. Question:

_____
_____

Research Chemists analyze the chemical
makeup of matter and investigate how
to develop new products from raw
materials. Question:

_____
_____
_____
_____

Lab zone® Do the Lab Investigation
Piecing Information Together.

🔑 Assess Your Understanding

1a. Identify Give an example of a scientific
problem that involves scientists from
different fields working together.

_____
_____
_____

b. Apply Concepts How might a life scientist
contribute to the study of volcanoes?

_____
_____
_____

got it?

○ **I get it!** Now I know that scientists in different
fields work together because _____
_____
_____
_____

○ **I need extra help with** _____

Go to **my science** ⓢ **coach** *online for help with
this subject.*

57

How Is Science Important in Non-Science Careers?

Are scientists the only people who need knowledge of science on the job? The answer, of course, is no. 🔑 **In many non-science careers, knowledge of science is essential to perform the job.** A few careers that involve science are shown in **Figure 5**.

FIGURE 5 ·······················
> **INTERACTIVE ART** **Careers and Science**
Most people need to know some science to do their jobs.

✎ **Read about each career. Then answer the question in each box.**

Artists use science. Glass artists apply heat to shape glass. Sculptors need to identify good material for outdoor sculptures.
✎ **Apply Concepts Identify the area of science that one of these artists uses. Then explain how the artist uses it.**

_____
_____
_____
_____

Chefs rely on science whether they are working in restaurants, hotels, or school cafeterias. They need to know chemistry because cooking involves chemical change. They must know life science to prevent food from spoiling.
✎ **Identify Describe what other areas of life science chefs must know about and why.**

_____
_____

Auto Repair Technicians need to know the physics of engines and the chemistry of fuels and fluids to fix cars. They also use scientific thinking and scientific skills such as observation.
✎ **Infer Explain why knowing about electricity would help an auto repair technician.**

_____
_____
_____

apply it!

Firefighters need to know science to help put out fires and save lives.

1 ◭ **Communicate** Discuss with a partner how firefighters use science. Write two examples. Identify the area of science that each example belongs to.

_____

_____

_____

_____

_____

2 Draw Conclusions Why is it important for firefighters to know some life, Earth, and physical science?

_____

_____

3 [CHALLENGE] What scientific principles do the adults in your family need to know to do their jobs?

_____

_____

_____

 Do the Quick Lab
Help Wanted.

🔑 Assess Your Understanding

2a. Review Why should everyone study some science?

_____

_____

_____

_____

b. Apply Concepts How would a knowledge of science benefit a gardener?

_____

_____

_____

got it?

○ **I get it!** Now I know that science is important to non-science careers because _____

_____

_____

_____

_____

_____

○ I need extra help with _____

Go to **MY SCIENCE ⓢ COACH** *online for help with this subject.*

REVIEW THE BIG

?

_____ and _____ are interconnected. What happens in one area affects what happens in the other.

LESSON 1 Why Study Science?

🔑 Understanding scientific principles and thinking scientifically can help you solve problems and answer questions throughout your life.

Vocabulary
• cost
• benefit

LESSON 2 Scientific Literacy

🔑 By having scientific literacy, you will be able to identify good sources of scientific information, evaluate them for accuracy, and apply the knowledge to questions or problems in your life.

🔑 You can use scientific reasoning to analyze scientific claims by looking for bias and errors in the research, evaluating data, and identifying faulty reasoning.

🔑 To make decisions and design experiments, you need relevant and reliable background information.

Vocabulary
• scientific literacy • evidence • opinion

LESSON 3 Scientists and Society

🔑 The work that scientists do changes society. In turn, society influences the work of scientists.

Vocabulary
• controversy

LESSON 4 Careers in Science

🔑 The three main areas of science careers are life science, earth and space science, and physical science.

🔑 Most scientists work in teams with scientists from other fields, because most scientific questions involve many fields of science.

🔑 In many non-science careers, knowledge of science is essential to perform the job.

Vocabulary • life science
• earth and space science • physical science

Review and Assessment

Why Study Science?

1. A positive consequence of an action is called a

   a. cost.   **b.** benefit.

   c. product.   **d.** principle.

2. A _____ is a negative result of taking or not taking an action.

3. Analyze Costs and Benefits Describe one cost and one benefit of recycling plastic at your school.

_____

_____

_____

_____

_____

4. Evaluate Scientific Claims An environmental group issued a press release claiming that a nearby river has been heavily polluted by a local chemical plant. Yet, the river doesn't look polluted. This environmental group is new, and no one has heard of it before. Why would a person need to know something about science to judge the validity of this group's claim?

_____

_____

_____

_____

_____

_____

_____

5. [Write About It] Design a five-panel comic strip that illustrates the importance of science education. Your comic strip should show a particular situation in which knowledge of science would have been important.

Scientific Literacy

6. Being able to understand basic scientific terms and principles well enough to apply them to your life is called

   a. evidence.   **b.** opinion.

   c. scientific literacy.   **d.** scientific questioning.

7. When you perform scientific research, you should look for information that is _____

8. Pose Questions A scientific study proves that frozen fruit is more nutritious than canned fruit. What questions would you want answered before you accept this claim?

_____

_____

_____

_____

9. Evaluate Data Reliability You are working on a science fair project and need to gather research on your topic. Where will you look for reliable information? Identify at least three different sources.

_____

_____

_____

_____

_____

_____

World Wide Web

File   Edit   View   Help

http://www.

| Water Usage | Search |

All About Water Use
How much do you know about the water you use? Take this quiz. By Mr. Pickle's 6th-Grade Class

Effect of Water Rate Increases on Reducing Water Usage in Sydney
NSW Government, Australia

Water Usage by County
Your State Government Office of Water Resources and Conservation

LESSON 3 **Scientists and Society**

10. The scientist who said that Earth moves around the sun is

   a. Rachel Carson.

   b. Galileo Galilei.

   c. Albert Einstein.

   d. Ignaz Semmelweis.

11. A public disagreement between groups with different views is called a _____

12. Evaluate Science in the Media Identify a scientific controversy that you have seen reported on television, in a newspaper or magazine, or on the Internet.

_____

_____

_____

13. Evaluate the Impact on Society How do you think Ignaz Semmelweis's discovery in the 1840s impacts modern medicine?

_____

_____

_____

_____

_____

_____

14. Write About It A company must clear the land of existing trees in order to erect a new building. Some people support the company because the expansion will provide new jobs. Other people are against it because they don't want the wildlife to be destroyed. On a separate sheet of paper, write which side of the controversy you would support and why.

LESSON 4 **Careers in Science**

15. The study of Earth and its place in the universe is

   a. life science.   **b.** computer science.

   c. earth and space science.   **d.** physical science.

16. _____ includes the study of motion, sound, light, electricity, and magnetism.

17. Make Generalizations If your friend wants to become an astronaut, does she need to study only space science? Why or why not?

_____

_____

_____

_____

APPLY THE BIG ❓ How do science and society affect each other?

18. Explain how the invention of cell phones has affected today's society. What might daily life have been like before cell phones were invented? How have things changed since cell phones were created?

_____

_____

_____

_____

_____

_____

_____

_____

Standardized Test Prep

Multiple Choice

Circle the letter of the best answer.

The graph below compares how well two different brands of insulated mugs retain heat. Use the graph to answer Question 1.

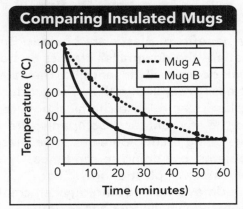

Comparing Insulated Mugs

1. The information contained in the graph is an example of
   A bias.
   B evidence.
   C opinion.
   D reasoning.

2. What would be the best way to determine which brand of paper towels is the strongest when wet?
   A comparing television commercials that demonstrate the strength of paper towels
   B tearing different brands of towels when they are wet to feel which seems strongest
   C comparing how much weight each brand of towel can hold when wet before it breaks
   D asking chefs which brand is best

3. A public disagreement between groups with different views is called
   A faulty reasoning.
   B a controversy.
   C a decision.
   D reliable data.

4. What is a negative consequence of either taking or not taking an action called?
   A an impact
   B a benefit
   C a principle
   D a cost

5. A volcanologist studies volcanoes. This is an example of
   A earth and space science.
   B life science.
   C computer science.
   D physical science.

Constructed Response

Use the image below and your knowledge of science to help you answer Question 6. Write your answer on a separate sheet of paper.

6. What are three scientific questions the creators of this roller coaster might have asked when designing it? Why are these questions important?

BAKELITE®:
Molding the Future

In 1907, Dr. Leo Baekeland created the first artificial plastic. Bakelite, as he called it, was an instant hit. It was strong and didn't easily melt. It could be molded into any shape in any color. At the time, more and more people were using electricity. Bakelite did not conduct electricity, so it was an excellent insulator. It was used to make electric plugs and cases for electronic devices like telephones.

Soon, Bakelite was everywhere. People found a lot of uses for such a valuable yet inexpensive material. It was used to make everything from engine parts to jewelry. And that was just the beginning.

Later, chemists created other, more useful types of plastic. Now over a century later, can you imagine life without plastic?

The benefits of plastic are obvious. But what are the downfalls? Plastics do not break down easily in landfills. They are not easily recycled, either. The production of plastic can release chemical pollutants into the environment. Companies are developing technologies to solve these problems, but doing so can be costly. The history of plastic shows that sometimes a new technology can create unforeseen challenges for society.

Analyze It Working with a partner, choose a new technology. Learn about the benefits and drawbacks of this technology. Then, do a cost-benefit analysis.

CAFFEINE CAUSES HALLUCINATIONS!

A new study reports that the equivalent of seven cups of coffee a day could cause people to see "ghosts."

Reading Between the Lines

Headlines grab your attention. That's their job—to get you to read more. Sometimes, though, when headlines promise interesting news, the report doesn't deliver accurate scientific data.

Recently, some newspapers reported that caffeine caused people to hallucinate. The report cited a study that showed that people who drank seven or more cups of coffee in a day saw things that weren't really there.

The newspapers reported the results of the study because a lot of people drink coffee and tea, which both have caffeine. So, a lot of people would find the study interesting. However, the study had some flaws.

It had a small sample of only 219 people. Also, the sample came from a specific group of people—university students. The study took the form of a survey, which means the researchers did not directly observe the subjects. Finally, the researchers did not have a control group. There was no way for them to determine if other factors, besides the caffeine, had affected the subjects. Many scientists later agreed that more tests still needed to be done.

Science doesn't always make for interesting news. Most scientific discoveries happen slowly. They are the result of many trials performed over long periods of time. So be critical of catchy headlines that promise an interesting story. You may not be reading accurate science.

Analyze It Compare articles about science in two or three news sources. Are the headlines more eye-catching in one source? Identify the science claims that the articles make. Identify the evidence that supports these claims. Which source provides the clearest evidence? Which source relies mostly on opinions and assumptions? Create a table to compare the reporting in your sources.

WHY ARE THESE SCIENTISTS WEIGHING A POLAR BEAR?

How is mathematics important to the work of scientists?

Scientists weighed this small female polar bear while she was asleep. They also measured the bear's body and skull. Similar measurements were done on bears throughout the Beaufort Sea of Alaska. The bears live on a frozen portion of the ocean called sea ice. Scientists are also measuring the sea ice to determine how much the ice is shrinking. By taking these measurements, scientists can figure out how the bears are affected by their environment.

> UNTAMED SCIENCE Watch the **Untamed Science** video to learn more about how tools help scientists.

Develop Hypotheses **Write a hypothesis that could be tested with these scientists' measurements.**

_____

_____

_____

3 Getting Started

Check Your Understanding

1. **Background** Read the paragraph below and then answer the question.

> Emi studied hard to prepare for her science lab investigation. Emi was concerned because her investigation was **complex.** She had been earning high marks all year and wanted to maintain this **trend.** Emi also wanted to use her lab report as a **sample** of her science work.

> To be **complex** is to have many parts.
>
> A **trend** is the general direction that something tends to move.
>
> A **sample** is a portion of something that is used to represent the whole thing.

• Why would preparing help Emi maintain her high marks?

_____

_____

> **MY READING WEB** If you had trouble completing the question above, visit **My Reading Web** and type in *The Tools of Science.*

Vocabulary Skill

Identify Multiple Meanings Some words have more than one meaning. The table below lists multiple meaning words used in science and in daily life.

Word	Everyday Meaning	Scientific Meaning
mean	*v.* to indicate; to intend **Example:** They didn't *mean* to hurt her.	*n.* the numerical average **Example:** The *mean* of 11, 7, 5, and 9 is 8.
volume	*n.* the loudness of a sound **Example:** Turn up the *volume* so we can hear the song.	*n.* the amount of space an object or substance takes up **Example:** Record the *volume* of water in the graduated cylinder.

2. **Quick Check** In the table above, circle the meaning of the word *volume* that is used in the following sentence.

• The *volume* of juice in the container is 1.89 liters.

density

accuracy

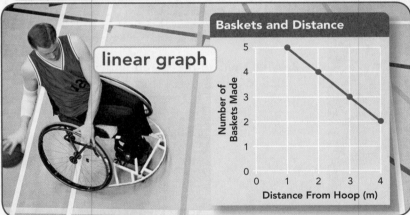

linear graph

Baskets and Distance

(graph: Number of Baskets Made vs. Distance From Hoop (m), y-axis 0–5, x-axis 0–4)

safety symbols

Chapter Preview

LESSON 1

- metric system • SI
- mass • weight • volume
- meniscus • density

↻ **Compare and Contrast**

△ **Measure**

LESSON 2

- estimate • accuracy
- precision • significant figures
- percent error • mean
- median • mode • range
- anomalous data

↻ **Relate Cause and Effect**

△ **Calculate**

LESSON 3

- graph • linear graph
- nonlinear graph

↻ **Relate Text and Visuals**

△ **Predict**

LESSON 4

- model • system • input
- process • output • feedback

↻ **Identify the Main Idea**

△ **Make Models**

LESSON 5

- safety symbol
- field

↻ **Summarize**

△ **Observe**

> **VOCAB FLASH CARDS** For extra help with vocabulary, visit **Vocab Flash Cards** and type in *The Tools of Science.*

Measurement— A Common Language

🔑 Why Do Scientists Use a Standard Measurement System?

🔑 What Are Some SI Units of Measure?

mY pLaNeT DiaRY

Extreme Measurements

Here are some fascinating animal measurements.

- The Queen Alexandra's Birdwing butterfly has a wingspan of 30 centimeters.
- A newborn giraffe stands 1.8 meters tall.
- When a blue whale exhales, the spray from its blowhole can reach up to 9 meters into the air.
- A colossal squid's eye measures about 28 centimeters across.
- With a mass of only 20 grams, the rhinoceros beetle can lift 850 times its own mass.
- A hummingbird's egg has a mass of about half a gram while an ostrich egg has a mass of about 1,500 grams.

Ostrich egg

FUN FACTS

Read the following questions. Write your answers below.

1. What problems could arise if some scientists measured length in inches and others measured length in centimeters?

_____

_____

_____

2. What units of measurement would you use to measure your height and mass?

_____

_____

_____

_____

> PLANET DIARY Go to **Planet Diary** to learn more about measurement.

Lab zone® Do the Inquiry Warm-Up *History of Measurement.*

Hummingbird eggs

Vocabulary

- metric system • SI • mass • weight
- volume • meniscus • density

Skills

- Reading: Compare and Contrast
- Inquiry: Measure

Why Do Scientists Use a Standard Measurement System?

Standard measurement is important. Without it, cooks would use handfuls and pinches instead of cups and tablespoons.

Scientists also use standard measurements. This allows scientists everywhere to repeat experiments. In the 1790s, scientists in France developed the metric system of measurement. The **metric system** is a measurement system based on the number 10. Modern scientists use a version of the metric system called the International System of Units, or **SI** (from the French, *Système International d'Unités*). **Using SI as the standard system of measurement allows scientists to compare data and communicate with each other about their results.** The prefixes used in the SI system are shown in **Figure 1.**

FIGURE 1 ·······················

> VIRTUAL LAB **SI Prefixes**

SI units are similar to our money units, in which a dime is ten times more than a penny.

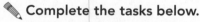 **Complete the tasks below.**

1. **Name** In the table at the right, finish filling in the Example column.

2. **Calculate** How many times larger is a *kilo-* than a *deka-*?

_____

_____

Common SI Prefixes

Prefix	Meaning	Example
kilo- (k)	1,000	_____
hecto- (h)	100	_____
deka- (da)	10	dekameter
no prefix	1	meter
deci- (d)	0.1 (one tenth)	_____
centi- (c)	0.01 (one hundredth)	_____
milli- (m)	0.001 (one thousandth)	_____

Lab zone® Do the Quick Lab *How Many Shoes?*

Assess Your Understanding

got it? ···

○ **I get it!** Now I know that scientists use a standard measurement system to _____

_____

○ **I need extra help with** _____

Go to **my science COACH** *online for help with this subject.*

What Are Some SI Units of Measure?

Scientists regularly measure attributes such as length, mass, volume, density, temperature, and time. Each attribute is measured in an SI unit.

Length Length is the distance from one point to another. 🔑 **In SI, the basic unit for measuring length is the meter (m).** Many distances can be measured in meters. For example, you can measure a softball throw or your height in meters. One meter is about the distance from the floor to a doorknob. A tool used to measure length is a metric ruler.

For measuring lengths smaller than a meter, you use the centimeter (cm) and millimeter (mm). For example, the length of this page is about 28 centimeters. For measuring a long distance, such as the distance between cities, you use the unit called a kilometer (km). The table at the left shows you how to convert between different metric length units. Try measuring the turtle's shell in **Figure 2**.

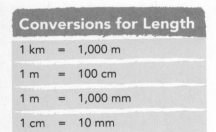

Conversions for Length		
1 km	=	1,000 m
1 m	=	100 cm
1 m	=	1,000 mm
1 cm	=	10 mm

FIGURE 2 ···

Measuring Length

To use a metric ruler, line up one end of an object with the zero mark. Then read the number at the object's other end.

✏️ **Use the ruler to measure the length of the turtle's shell and record it above the arrow. Then working in small groups, complete the activity below.**

Length =

1. **Measure** Measure the width of a penny and a dime in millimeters.

   _____

   _____

2. **Calculate** Convert the width of each coin in millimeters into centimeters.

   _____

   _____

   _____

The centimeter markings are the longer lines. Each centimeter is divided into 10 millimeters, which are marked by the shorter lines.

cm

Mass A balance, such as the one shown in **Figure 3,** is used to measure mass. **Mass** is a measure of the amount of matter in an object. A balance compares the mass of an object to a known mass. 🔑 **In SI, the basic unit for measuring mass is the kilogram (kg).** The mass of cars, bicycles, and people is measured in kilograms. If you want to measure much smaller masses, you would use grams (g) or milligrams (mg). The table at the right shows how to convert between kilograms, grams, and milligrams.

Unlike mass, **weight** is a measure of the force of gravity acting on an object. A scale is used to measure weight. When you stand on a scale on Earth, gravity pulls you downward. This compresses springs inside the scale. The more you weigh, the more the springs compress. On the moon, the force of gravity is weaker than it is on Earth. So the scale's springs would not compress as much on the moon as on Earth. Unlike weight, your mass on the moon is the same as your mass on Earth.

Conversions for Mass

1 kg	=	1,000 g
1 g	=	1,000 mg

✏️ **Compare and Contrast**
Use the chart to compare and contrast mass and weight.

Alike	Different

FIGURE 3 ······················

Measuring Mass
A triple-beam balance can be used to measure mass.

✏️ **Measure** Read the balance to find the mass of the turtle. Record your answer in grams and then in milligrams.

_____

_____

1 Place an object on the pan.

2 Shift the riders on the beams until they balance the object and the pointer hits 0.

3 Add up the grams shown on all three beams to find the mass.

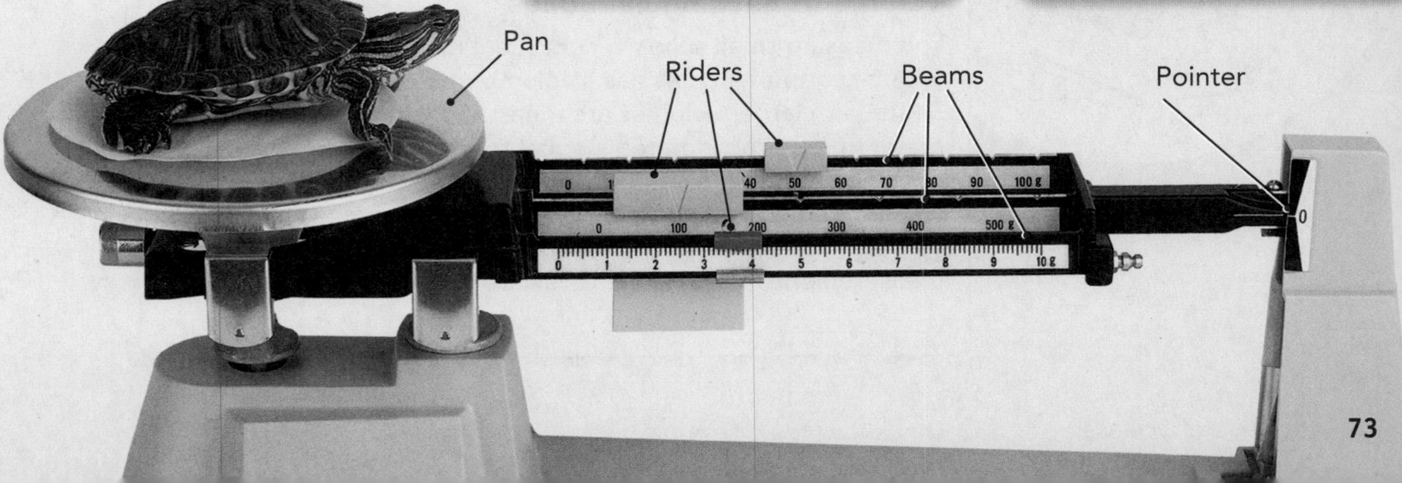

Pan

Riders

Beams

Pointer

0   10   40   50   60   70   80   90   100 g

0   100   200   300   400   500 g

0   1   2   3   4   5   6   7   8   9   10 g

Conversions for Volume

1 m³	=	1,000,000 cm³
1 cm³	=	1 mL
1 L	=	1,000 mL
1 L	=	1,000 cm³

Volume Instead of measuring your juice, you just look to see how much of the glass you have filled up. **Volume** is the amount of space an object or substance takes up. 🔑 **In SI, the basic unit for measuring volume is the cubic meter (m³).** Other units include the liter (L) and the cubic centimeter (cm³). Cubic meters or centimeters are used to measure the volume of solids. The liter is commonly used for measuring the volume of liquids. The green table shows how to convert between these units.

FIGURE 4 ···

Volume of Liquids, Rectangular Solids, and Irregular Solids

Measuring the volume of liquids and rectangular solids requires different methods.

✏️ **Complete the activity on this page. Then follow the steps to measure the volume of an irregular solid on the next page.**

Explain In the boxes, find the volume of the liquid and the cereal box. Below, explain which has a greater volume.

_____

_____

_____

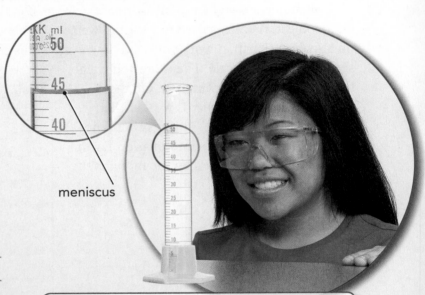

meniscus

Volume of Liquids

You are probably familiar with the liter from seeing 1-liter and 2-liter bottles. You can measure smaller liquid volumes by using milliliters (mL). There are 1,000 milliliters in one liter. To measure the volume of a liquid, read the level at the bottom of the **meniscus,** or curve. What is the volume of this liquid?

_____

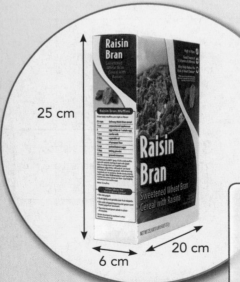

25 cm

20 cm

6 cm

Volume of Rectangular Solids

You measure small solids in cubic centimeters (cm³). A cube with 1-centimeter sides has a volume of 1 cubic centimeter. Solids with larger volumes are measured with the cubic meter (m³). A cubic meter is equal to the volume of a cube with 1-meter sides. To calculate a rectangular solid's volume, multiply length times width times height. When you use this formula, you must use the same units for all measurements. What is the cereal box's volume?

_____

Volume of Irregular Solids

Suppose you wanted to measure the volume of a rock. Because of its irregular shape, you cannot measure a rock's length, width, or height. However, you can use the displacement method shown on this page. To use this method, you immerse the object in water and measure how much the water level rises.

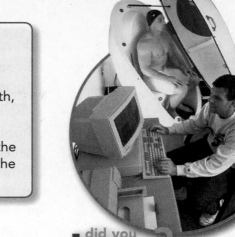

Athletes may have their body volume measured to calculate their density, which can be used to determine their body fat percentage. One method for measuring an athlete's volume involves displacement of air by the athlete in an airtight device.

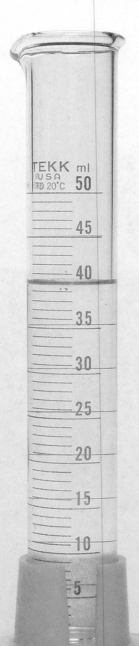

1 Fill a graduated cylinder about two thirds full of water.

What is the volume of water in the graduated cylinder?

_____

2 Place the object into the water.

What is the volume of the water plus the object?

_____

3 Find the volume of the object by subtracting the volume of the water alone from the volume of the water plus the object.

What is the volume of the object?

_____

Density Look at **Figure 5.** Two objects of the same size can have different masses. This is because different materials have different densities. **Density** is a measure of how much mass is contained in a given volume.

Units of Density Because density is made up of two measurements, mass and volume, an object's density is expressed as a relationship between two units.  **In SI, the basic unit for measuring density is kilograms per cubic meter (kg/m³).** Other units of density are grams per cubic centimeter (g/cm³) and grams per milliliter (g/mL).

FIGURE 5 ··

Comparing Densities
The bowling ball and the beach ball have the same volume but not the same mass.

✎ **Form Operational Definitions** Use this information to decide which object has a greater density. Explain your answer in terms of volume and mass.

_____

_____

_____

do the
math!

Calculating Density

The density of an object is the object's mass divided by its volume. To find the density of an object, use the formula below.

$$\text{Density} = \frac{\text{mass}}{\text{volume}}$$

❶ Calculate Find the density of a piece of metal that has a mass of 68 g and a volume of 6 cm³.

_____

❷ Predict Suppose a piece of metal has the same mass as the metal in Question 1 but a greater volume. How would its density compare to the metal in Question 1?

_____

_____

Density of Substances The table in **Figure 6** lists the densities of some common substances. The density of a pure substance is the same for all samples of that substance. For example, all samples of pure gold, no matter how large or small, have a density of 19.3 g/cm^3.

Once you know an object's density, you can determine whether the object will float in a given liquid. An object will float if it is less dense than the surrounding liquid. For example, the density of water is 1 g/cm^3. A piece of wood with a density of 0.8 g/cm^3 will float in water. A ring made of pure silver, which has a density of 10.5 g/cm^3, will sink.

FIGURE 6 ···

A Density Experiment
Knowing the density of an object helps you predict how it will float and identify what it is made of.

✎ **Complete the tasks below.**

1. **Infer** An object has a density of 0.7 g/cm^3. Do you think it floats or sinks in water? Explain.

   _____

   _____

2. **Design Experiments** Use what you know about density and measuring tools to describe the steps you might use to determine if a bar of metal is gold. Write your procedure in the notebook.

Densities of Some Common Substances	
Substance	**Density (g/cm³)**
Air	0.001
Ice	0.9
Water	1.0
Aluminum	2.7
Gold	19.3

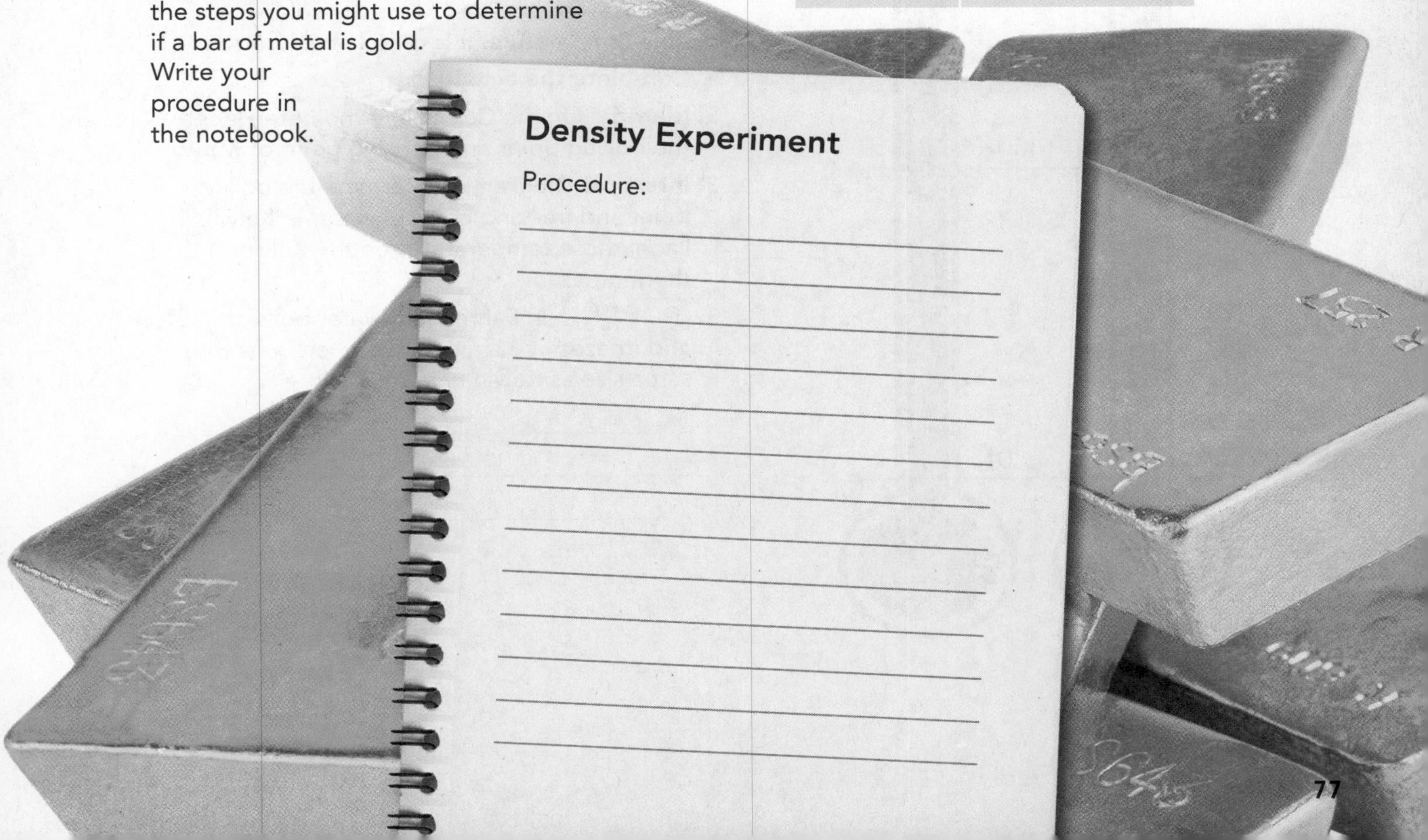

Density Experiment
Procedure:

_____

_____

_____

_____

_____

_____

_____

_____

_____

_____

_____

_____

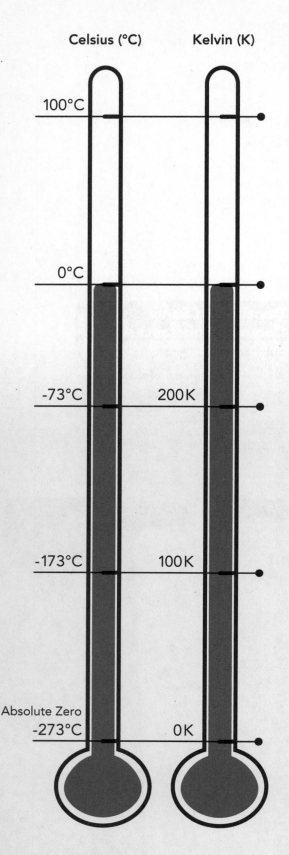

Celsius (°C) Kelvin (K)

100°C

0°C

-73°C   200 K

-173°C   100 K

Absolute Zero
-273°C   0 K

Temperature
Is it cold out this morning? How high will the temperature rise? You probably use temperature measurements often in your everyday life. So do scientists.

Scientists commonly use the Celsius temperature scale to measure temperature. On the Celsius scale, water freezes at 0°C and boils at 100°C. **In addition to the Celsius scale, scientists sometimes use another temperature scale, called the Kelvin scale. In fact, the kelvin (K) is the official SI unit for temperature.** Kelvin is useful in science because there are no negative numbers. Units on the Kelvin scale are the same size as those on the Celsius scale, as shown in **Figure 7.** The table below shows how to convert between Celsius and Kelvin.

A thermometer is used to measure temperature. When you place a liquid thermometer in a substance, the liquid inside the thermometer will increase or decrease in volume. This makes the level rise or fall. Wait until the level stops changing. Then read the number next to the top of the liquid in the thermometer.

FIGURE 7 ···
Temperature Scales
Zero on the Kelvin scale (0 K) is the coldest possible temperature. It is called absolute zero.

✎ **Complete the activities.**

1. **Identify** On the Celsius thermometer, label the boiling point and freezing point of water.

2. **Interpret Diagrams** Determine the boiling point and freezing point of water in Kelvins. Label these temperatures on the Kelvin thermometer.

3. **CHALLENGE** In Fahrenheit, water boils at 212° and freezes at 32°. Are Fahrenheit units the same size as Kelvin units? Explain.

_____

_____

_____

Conversions for Temperature

0°C	=	273 K
100°C	=	373 K

Time You push to run even faster with the finish line in sight. But an opponent is catching up. Just one second can mean the difference between winning and losing. What is a second?

🔑 **The second (s) is the SI unit used to measure time.** Just like all the SI units, the second is divided into smaller units based on the number 10. For example, a millisecond (ms) is one thousandth of a second. You use minutes or hours for longer periods of time. There are 60 seconds in a minute, and 60 minutes in an hour.

Clocks and watches are used to measure time. Some clocks are more accurate than others. Most digital stopwatches measure time accurately to one hundredth of a second, as shown in **Figure 8**. Devices used for timing Olympic events measure time to a thousandth of a second or even closer.

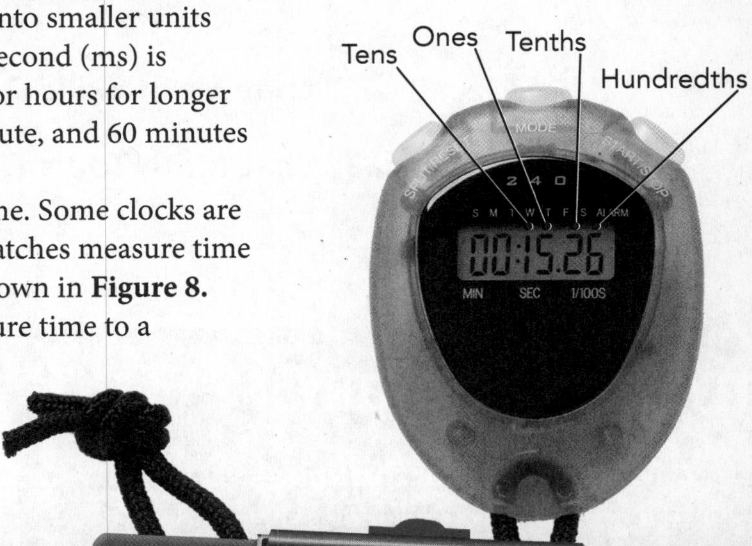

Tens Ones Tenths Hundredths

00:15.26

MIN   SEC   1/100S

FIGURE 8 ···

It's About Time
This stopwatch measured Jessie's best time in a school race.

✏️ **Write Jessie's time in the chart and then complete the activity.**

Interpret Tables In the last column, write the order that the runners finished.

Runner	Time	Place
George	00:15.74	
Sarah	00:26.78	
Saul	00:20.22	
Jessie		

Lab zone Do the Quick Lab
Measuring Length in Metric.

🔑 **Assess Your Understanding**

1a. Identify What tool would you use to measure the mass of a baseball?

_____

_____

b. Sequence What steps would you take to determine the density of a baseball?

_____

_____

_____

_____

_____

got it?

○ **I get it!** Now I know that basic SI units of

measurement are _____

_____

_____

_____

○ **I need extra help with** _____

Go to MY SCIENCE ⓢ COACH *online for help with this subject.*

Mathematics and Science

UNLOCK THE BIG ?

🔑 **What Math Skills Do Scientists Use?**

🔑 **What Math Tools Do Scientists Use?**

MY PLANET DiARY

Measuring Earthquakes

The ground shakes, windows shatter, debris falls from above, and the streets are crowded with screaming people. This is how earthquakes are often depicted in the media. However, not all earthquakes cause such chaos and destruction. Some are so small they aren't even felt.

Since earthquakes occur all over the world, scientists must use a universal system of measurement to compare them. For large earthquakes, scientists use a measurement known as the moment magnitude scale. As the number on the scale increases, so does the size of the earthquake. So far, the largest earthquake on record occurred in Chile in 1960 and measured 9.5 on the moment magnitude scale.

DISCOVERY

Communicate Discuss the following question with a partner. Write your answer below.

What do you know about earthquakes? How can you stay safe during one?

_____
_____
_____
_____
_____
_____
_____

▶ PLANET DIARY Go to **Planet Diary** to learn more about mathematics and science.

Lab zone® Do the Inquiry Warm-Up *How Many Marbles Are There?*

Vocabulary

- estimate • accuracy • precision
- significant figures • percent error • mean
- median • mode • range • anomalous data

Skills

↻ **Reading:** Relate Cause and Effect

△ **Inquiry:** Calculate

What Math Skills Do Scientists Use?

From measuring to collecting data, scientists use math every day. 🔑 **Math skills that scientists use to collect data include estimation, accuracy and precision, and significant figures.**

Estimation An **estimate** is an approximation of a number based on reasonable assumptions. An estimate is not a guess. It is always based on known information. Scientists often rely on estimates when they cannot obtain exact numbers. Their estimates might be based on indirect measurements, calculations, and models. For example, they may estimate the distance between stars based on indirect measurements because they can't measure the distance directly. Other estimates might be based on a sample.

do the math!

Estimation

Estimating from a sample is a quick way to determine the large number of birds in this photo.

1 **Interpret Photos** How many birds are in the yellow square? This number is your sample.

_____

2 **Explain** By what number should you multiply the sample to find an estimate for the total number of birds in the total area? Explain your answer.

_____

_____

_____

3 **Estimate** Calculate your estimate for the total number of birds. Show your work.

_____

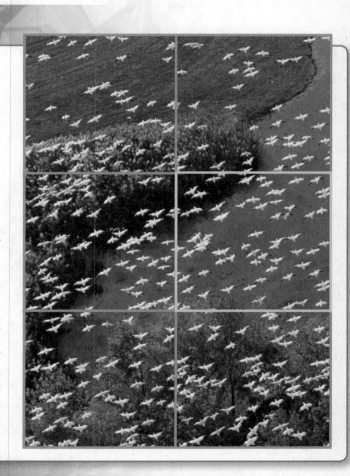

Accuracy and Precision

People often use the words *accuracy* and *precision* to describe the same idea. In science, these words have different meanings. **Accuracy** refers to how close a measurement is to the true or accepted value. **Precision** refers to how close a group of measurements are to each other.

How can you be sure that a measurement is both accurate and precise? First, use a high-quality measurement tool. Second, measure carefully. Finally, repeat the measurement a few times. If your measurement is the same each time, you can assume that it is reliable. A reliable measurement is both accurate and precise. Look at **Figure 1**.

FIGURE 1 ·····················

Accuracy and Precision

In a game of darts, accurate throws land close to the bull's eye. Precise throws land close to one another.

✎ **Apply Concepts** Draw dots on boards C and D to show the situations described.

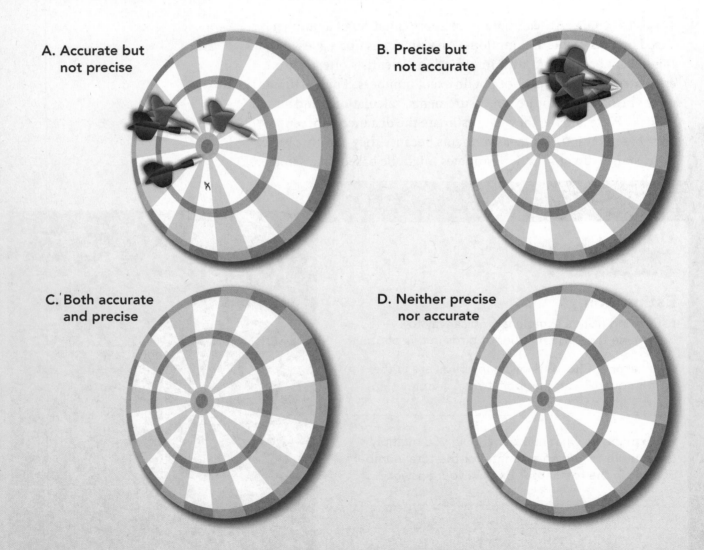

A. Accurate but not precise

B. Precise but not accurate

C. Both accurate and precise

D. Neither precise nor accurate

Significant Figures

Significant figures communicate how precise measurements are. The **significant figures** in a measurement include all digits measured exactly, plus one estimated digit. If the measurement has only one digit, you must assume it is estimated. Use **Figure 2** to learn more about significant figures.

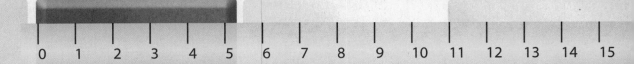

0 1 2 3 4 5 6 7 8 9 10 11 12 13 14 15

Adding or Subtracting Measurements

When you add or subtract measurements, your answer can only have as many places after the decimal point as the measurement with the fewest places after the decimal point. For example, suppose you add a tile that is 5.3 centimeters long to a row of tiles that is 21.94 centimeters long. Find the new length of the row.

```
  21.94 cm (2 places after the decimal)
+  5.3  cm (1 place after the decimal)
  27.24 cm → 27.2 cm (1 place after the decimal)
```

If you remove a tile that is 5.3 centimeters long from a row of tiles that is 21.94 centimeters long, what is the new length of the row? How many significant figures are in this measurement?

_____

_____

FIGURE 2 ·······················
Significant Figures

Suppose you are tiling a bathroom. You might estimate that the tile is 5.3 cm long. The measurement 5.3 cm has two significant figures, or sig figs. You are certain of the 5, but you have estimated the 3.

✎ **Calculate Read about adding, subtracting, and multiplying measurements. Then complete the activities in the boxes.**

Multiplying Measurements

When you multiply measurements, the answer should only have the same number of significant figures as the measurement with the fewest significant figures. For example, suppose you need to find the area of a space that measures 2.25 meters by 3 meters.

```
  2.25 m  (3 sig figs)
×    3 m  (1 sig fig)
  6.75 m² → 7 m² (1 sig fig)
```

Find the area of a space that measures 4.4 meters by 2 meters. How many significant figures are in this measurement?

_____

_____

Do the Quick Lab
For Good Measure.

 Assess Your Understanding

1a. Review What math skill do scientists rely on when they cannot obtain exact numbers?

_____

_____

b. Interpret Data Lia measures a wall of her room to be 3.7 meters by 2.45 meters. How many significant figures are in the measurement of its area? Explain.

_____

_____

got it?

● **I get it!** Now I know that the math skills scientists use to collect data include _____

_____

_____

○ I need extra help with _____

Go to MY SCIENCE ⓢ COACH *online for help with this subject.*

What Math Tools Do Scientists Use?

Mathematics is just as powerful a tool for analyzing data as it is for collecting it. Scientists use certain math tools to analyze data. These tools include calculating percent error; finding the mean, median, mode, and range; and checking the reasonableness of data.

Percent Error   Often, scientists must make measurements that already have accepted values. For example, an accepted, or true, value for the density of the metal copper is 8.92 g/cm^3. Suppose you measure the mass and volume of a sample of the metal copper, and calculate a density of 9.37 g/cm^3. You know your calculation is not accurate, but by how much? **Percent error** calculations are a way to determine how accurate an experimental value is. A low percent error means that the result you obtained was accurate. A high percent error means that your result was not accurate. It may not be accurate because you did not measure carefully or something was wrong with your measurement tool.

Relate Cause and Effect
Underline the causes of a high percent error.

do the math! Sample Problem

Percent Error

The experimental density of copper is 9.37 g/cm^3. The true value is 8.92 g/cm^3. To calculate the percent error, use the following formula and substitute.

$$\text{Percent error} = \frac{\text{Difference between experimental value and true value}}{\text{true value}} \times 100\%$$

$$\%E = \frac{9.37 \text{ g/cm}^3 - 8.92 \text{ g/cm}^3}{8.92 \text{ g/cm}^3} \times 100\%$$

The percent error in the calculation of the density of copper was 5.04%.

❶ **Calculate** Suppose you measured the density of a silver ring to be 11.2 g/cm^3, but you know that the true value for the density of silver is 10.5 g/cm^3. Find the percent error for the density you measured.

_____

_____

_____

❷ **CHALLENGE** What are two possible sources of error when measuring a sample's mass and volume?

_____

_____

_____

Mean, Median, Mode, and Range

Walking along a beach one night, you see a sea turtle laying her eggs in the sand. You start to wonder about sea turtle nests. What is the average number of eggs in a nest? What is the range of eggs in a group of nests? Scientists ask questions like these, too. Their answers come from analyzing data. Use **Figure 3** to analyze sea turtle egg data yourself.

Mean The **mean** is the numerical average of a set of data. To find the mean, add up the numbers in the data set. Then divide the sum by the total number of items you added.

Find the mean for the egg data.

_____

Median The **median** is the middle number in a set of data. To find the median, list all the numbers in order from least to greatest. The median is the middle entry. If a list has an even number of entries, add the two middle numbers together and divide by two to find the median.

Find the median for the egg data.

_____

_____

Mode The **mode** is the number that appears most often in a list of numbers.

Find the mode for the egg data.

_____

Range The **range** of a set of data is the difference between the greatest value and the least value in the set.

Find the range for the egg data.

_____

FIGURE 3 ·······························

Sea Turtle Egg Data
You can use math to analyze the data in the table below about the number of sea turtle eggs in seven nests.

Calculate Fill in the boxes with the mean, median, mode, and range of the sea turtle data.

Nest	Number of Eggs
A	110
B	102
C	94
D	110
E	107
F	110
G	109

Sea Turtles at Nesting Beach

Day	Turtles
Day 1	7
Day 2	7
Day 3	8
Day 4	7
Day 5	2

FIGURE 4 ·······························

Collected Data
On Day 5, only two turtles are at the beach.

✎ **Analyze Experimental Results**
Describe an unknown variable that could have affected the data.

_____

_____

_____

_____

Reasonable and Anomalous Data An important part of analyzing any set of data is to ask, "Are these data reasonable? Do they make sense?" For example, suppose a scientist who studies sea turtles measures the ocean water temperature each night for five nights. His data for the first four nights are 26°C, 23°C, 25°C, and 24°C. On the last night, he asks a student to make the measurement. The student records 81 in the data book.

Are the data reasonable? The reading on Day 5 is very different. Some variation in ocean temperature makes sense within a small range. But it doesn't make sense for ocean temperature to rise 57°C in one day, from 24°C to 81°C. The 81°C does not fit with the rest of the data. Data that do not fit with the rest of a data set are **anomalous data.** In this case, the anomalous data are explainable. The student measured °F instead of °C. Sometimes asking whether data are reasonable can uncover sources of error or unknown variables. Investigating the reason for anomalous data can lead to new discoveries.

EXPLORE THE BIG ?

TURTLE TURF

How is mathematics important to the work of scientists?

THINK LIKE A SCIENTIST

FIGURE 5 ·······························

> INTERACTIVE ART Scientists use mathematics to help answer the question, "How and why are the number of sea turtle nests in Florida changing?"

✎ Design Experiments Answer the questions below.

The pale green coloring on the map shows areas where green sea turtles commonly nest in Florida.

1 How would you collect accurate and precise turtle nest data?

_____

_____

_____

2 What properties of the nests could you measure?

_____

_____

_____

_____

_____

3 How might a hurricane in Florida cause anamolous nest data?

_____

_____

4 How could you estimate the total number of nests in Florida?

_____

_____

_____

_____

_____

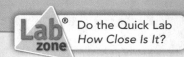
Do the Quick Lab
How Close Is It?

🔑 Assess Your Understanding

2a. Describe Why is it important for scientists to calculate percent error?

_____

_____

b. ANSWER THE BIG ❓ How is mathematics important to the work of scientists?

_____

_____

_____

_____

got it? ·······································

○ I get it! Now I know that math tools scientists use to analyze data include _____

_____

_____

_____

○ I need extra help with _____

Go to MY SCIENCE Ⓢ COACH *online for help with this subject.*

87

Graphs in Science

UNLOCK THE BIG ?Q

🔑 **What Kinds of Data Do Line Graphs Display?**

🔑 **Why Are Line Graphs Powerful Tools?**

MY PLANeT DiaRY

Waste and Recycling Data

The information below shows the amount of waste generated and recovered for recycling per person per day for each year listed.

- 1980: Generated waste was about 1.68 kg and recovered waste was about 0.16 kg.
- 1990: Generated waste was about 2.04 kg and recovered waste was about 0.33 kg.
- 2000: Generated waste was 2.09 kg and recovered waste was about 0.51 kg.
- 2002: Generated waste was about 2.09 kg and recovered waste was about 0.61 kg.
- 2007: Generated waste was about 2.09 kg and recovered waste was about 0.70 kg.

SCIENCE STATS

Communicate Discuss the following questions with a partner. Write your answers below.

How do you think society's view on recycling has changed over the years?

_____

_____

_____

_____

_____

PLANET DIARY Go to **Planet Diary** to learn more about graphs in science.

Lab zone® Do the Inquiry Warm-Up *What's in a Picture?*

What Kinds of Data Do Line Graphs Display?

Could the saying "A watched pot never boils" really be true? Or does it take longer to boil water when there is more water in the pot? You could do an experiment to find out. The table in **Figure 1** shows data from such an experiment. But what do the data mean? Does it take longer to boil a larger volume of water?

Vocabulary
• graph • linear graph • nonlinear graph

Skills
↻ Reading: Relate Text and Visuals
△ Inquiry: Predict

Line Graphs To help see what the data mean, you can use a graph. A **graph** is a "picture" of your data. One kind of graph is a line graph. ⚷ **Line graphs display data that show how one variable (the responding variable) changes in response to another variable (the manipulated variable).**

Using Line Graphs Scientists control changes in the manipulated variable. Then they collect data about how the responding variable changes. A line graph is used when a manipulated variable is continuous, which means there are other points between the tested ones. For example, in the water-boiling experiment, many volumes are possible between 500 mL and 2,000 mL.

FIGURE 1 ....

> INTERACTIVE ART **A Line Graph**
This line graph plots the data from the table below.

✎ **Identify** Identify the manipulated variable and the responding variable in the experiment.

_____

_____

_____

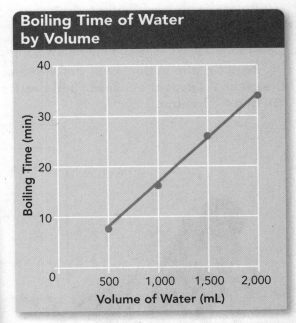

Boiling Time of Water by Volume

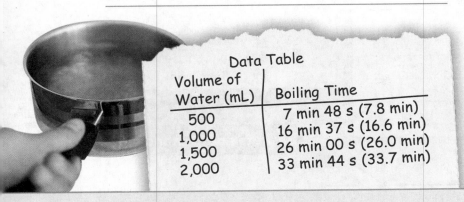

Data Table

Volume of Water (mL)	Boiling Time
500	7 min 48 s (7.8 min)
1,000	16 min 37 s (16.6 min)
1,500	26 min 00 s (26.0 min)
2,000	33 min 44 s (33.7 min)

Lab zone® Do the Quick Lab
What's a Line Graph?

⚷ Assess Your Understanding

got it? ....

○ I get it! Now I know that line graphs display data that _____

_____

○ I need extra help with _____

Go to MY SCIENCE ⓢ COACH online for help with this subject.

Why Are Line Graphs Powerful Tools?

A line graph in which the data points yield a straight line is a **linear graph.** The kind of graph in which the data points do not fall along a straight line is called a **nonlinear graph.** As shown in **Figure 2,** both kinds of line graphs are useful. 🔑 **Line graphs are powerful tools in science because they allow you to identify trends, make predictions, and recognize anomalous data.**

For example, the graph of experimental data in **Figure 3** on the next page shows that the trend is linear, even though most points do not fall exactly on the line. One point is clearly not part of the trend. It is an anomalous data point. Graphs make it easy to see anomalous data points like this one. When a graph does not have any clear trends, it probably means that the variables are not related.

✎ **Relate Text and Visuals**
Underline statements in the text that describe the graphs in Figure 2.

FIGURE 2 ....
Linear Trends
Data plotted in a line graph may show a trend.

✎ **Read Graphs** In the boxes, tell whether the graph is linear or nonlinear, and describe the graph's trend.

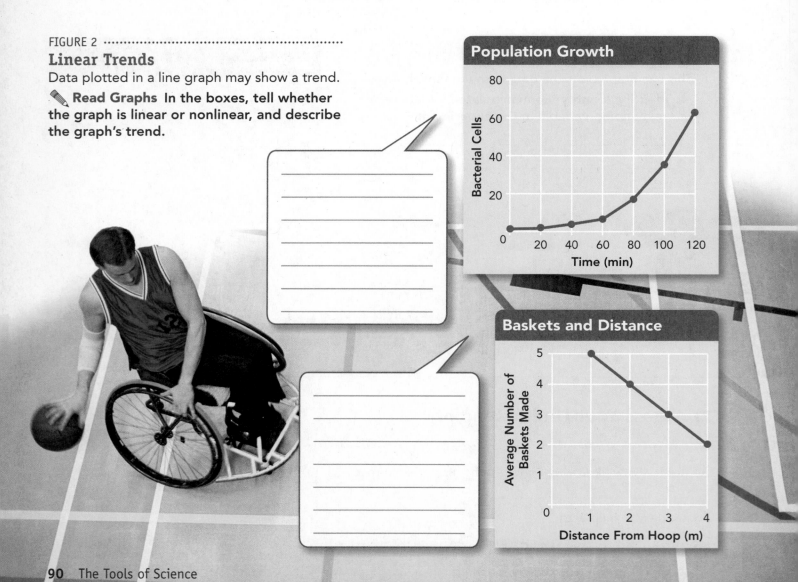

Population Growth

Baskets and Distance

Temperature of Heating Water

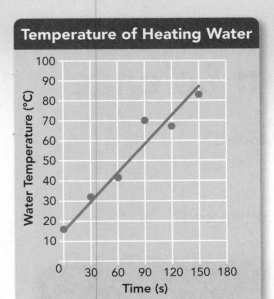

FIGURE 3 ....
Data Variation
Even though some points do not fall on the line, this graph shows a trend.

✎ **Complete the following tasks.**

1. **Identify** Label the anomalous data point.
2. **Predict** Use the graph to predict the temperature of the water after 180 seconds.

_____

apply it!

This graph shows the distance two friends biked in one hour.

❶ **Interpret Data** What is the relationship between the variables distance and time?

_____

❷ [CHALLENGE] During which time interval were the friends biking fastest? Explain.

_____
_____

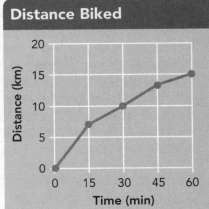

Distance Biked

Lab zone — Do the Lab Investigation *Density Graphs.*

🔑 Assess Your Understanding

1a. Review What does a graph with no trend show about the variables?

_____
_____

b. Compare and Contrast How does a graph with no trend differ from a graph with anomalous data points?

_____
_____

got it?

○ **I get it!** Now I know that line graphs are powerful tools because _____

_____
_____

○ **I need extra help with** _____

Go to **MY SCIENCE COACH** online for help with this subject.

Models as Tools in Science

UNLOCK
THE BIG
?

🔑 **Why Do Scientists Use Models?**

🔑 **What Is a System?**

🔑 **How Are Models of Systems Used?**

my pLaneT DiaRY

FUN FACTS

Flying Through Space

You don't have to be an astronaut to experience what it's like to fly in space. Thanks to technological advances, space flight simulation software programs have been created. These programs range from simple and straightforward to detailed and complicated. Depending on which one you use, you can experience what it might feel like to fly to the moon, command a mission to Mars, and even explore other solar systems. If you've ever wondered what it's like to be an astronaut, now you have the chance to find out!

Read the following questions. Write your answers below.

1. Why would a flight simulation software program created today be more realistic than one that was created ten years ago?

_____

_____

_____

_____

2. Would you be able to really fly in space if you knew how to use a space flight simulation software program? Explain.

_____

_____

_____

> PLANET DIARY Go to **Planet Diary** to learn more about models as tools in science.

Lab ® Do the Inquiry Warm-Up
zone *Scale Models.*

Inside a flight simulator

Vocabulary
- model • system • input
- process • output • feedback

Skills
⤺ **Reading: Identify the Main Idea**
△ **Inquiry: Make Models**

Why Do Scientists Use Models?

"Who is that model on the cover?" "I still have that model car I built." The word *model* has many meanings. But, as with many words, *model* has a specific meaning in science. In science, a **model** is any representation of an object or process. Pictures, diagrams, computer programs, and mathematical equations are all examples of scientific models.

🔑 **Scientists use models to understand things they cannot observe directly.** For example, scientists use models as reasonable representations of things that are either very large, such as Earth's core, or very small, such as an atom. These kinds of models are physical models—drawings or three-dimensional objects. Other models, such as mathematical equations or word descriptions, are models of processes. Look at the models in **Figure 1.**

FIGURE 1 ·······················

Two Science Models
Models may be three-dimensional objects or equations.

✎ **Explain** Tell whether each of these models represents an object or a process and why each is useful.

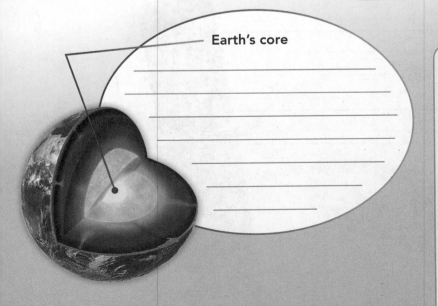

Photosynthesis

_____
_____
_____
_____

Carbon dioxide + Water —sunlight→ Food + Oxygen

Earth's core

_____
_____
_____
_____

Lab ® Do the Quick Lab
zone *Making Models.*

🔑 Assess Your Understanding

got it? ·····································

○ **I get it!** Now I know that scientists use

models to _____

_____

_____

○ **I need extra help with** _____

Go to **my science** ⓢ **coach** *online for help with this subject.*

What Is a System?

Many things you see and use are systems. For example, a toaster oven, your town's water pipes, and your bicycle are all systems. 🔑 **A system is a group of parts that work together to perform a function or produce a result.**

Systems have common properties. All systems have input, process, and output. **Input** is the material or energy that goes into a system. **Process** is what happens in a system. **Output** is the material or energy that comes out of a system. In addition, some systems have feedback. **Feedback** is output that changes the system in some way. For example, the heating and cooling system in most homes has feedback. A sensor in the thermostat recognizes when the desired temperature has been reached. The sensor provides feedback that turns the system off temporarily. Look at **Figure 2** to see another example of a system.

✏️ **Identify the Main Idea**
Circle the main idea in the second paragraph. Underline the details.

FIGURE 2 ···

An Everyday System
In a flashlight, many parts work together as a system.

✏️ **Apply Concepts** Look at the flashlight and use what you know to fill in the chart.

	Flashlight
Parts of System	
Input	
Process	
Output	

apply it!

Sun, air, land, and water are the parts of a system that produce a sea breeze. During the day, the sun's energy heats both the land and the water. The land and water, in turn, heat the air above them. Air over the land becomes much warmer than the air over water. As the warmer air rises, the cooler air from over the water rushes in to replace it. A sea breeze is the result.

An Afternoon Sea Breeze

1 Warm air rises

2 Cooler air moves to take warm air's place

Warm land

Cool water

❶ **Identify** Identify the input, output, and process of the sea breeze system.

_____
_____
_____
_____

❷ CHALLENGE Which parts of this system will change after the sun sets? How will it change?

_____
_____

 Do the Quick Lab Systems.

🔑 Assess Your Understanding

1a. List What are the properties of a system?

_____
_____
_____
_____

b. Apply Concepts A student uses a calculator to solve a math problem. Is this an example of a system? Explain your answer.

_____
_____
_____
_____

got it? ....

○ **I get it!** Now I know that a system is _____

_____
_____

○ **I need extra help with** _____

Go to MY SCIENCE ⑤ COACH online for help with this subject.

How Are Models of Systems Used?

It's easy to identify the materials and energy that make up the inputs and outputs of a system. It's not easy to observe a system's process. 🔑 **Scientists use models to understand how systems work. They also use models to predict changes in a system as a result of feedback or input changes.** However, they keep in mind that predictions based on models are uncertain.

When scientists construct a model of a system, they begin with certain assumptions. These assumptions allow them to make a basic model that accurately reflects the parts of the system and their relationships. A scientist who wants to study how energy moves through living things in an environment might use a model called a food chain. A food chain is a series that shows who eats whom to obtain energy in an environment. The food chain shown in **Figure 3** assumes that largemouth bass only eat flagfish. Largemouth bass actually eat many kinds of animals. However, the model still accurately reflects the relationship between the parts of a system.

Anhinga

Largemouth bass

Flagfish

Algae

FIGURE 3 ···

A Basic Model
In this model of a food chain in the Florida Everglades, the algae make food using the sun's energy. Algae are tiny living things that make their own food.

✏️ **Complete the tasks below.**

1. 🔺Make Models On the line next to each part of the system, write who eats it.

2. CHALLENGE What is the energy source for this system?

_____

The arrows show the direction in which energy moves. You can "read" an arrow as saying "are eaten by."

Flagfish: _____

Bass: _____

Algae: _____

Modeling a Simple System

A food chain is a good model to begin to understand how energy moves through living things in an environment. However, it shows how only a few of those living things are related. So a scientist may build a food web to model a more complete picture of the system. In **Figure 4** you can see a food web with many overlapping food chains. The food web is more detailed than one food chain. But it does not provide information about other factors, such as weather, that affect energy flow in the system.

FIGURE 4 ·····························

> INTERACTIVE ART **A Model of a Simple System**
This model of an Everglades food web contains overlapping food chains.

✎ **Interpret Diagrams** Study the food web model. On the notebook page write two things you learned from this complex model.

Alligator

Anhinga

Pig frog

Largemouth bass

Raccoon

Everglades crayfish

Flagfish

Plants, leaves, seeds, and fruits

Algae

97

Modeling a Complex System Some systems that scientists study are complex. Many parts and many variables interact in these systems. So scientists may use a computer to keep track of all the variables. Because such systems are difficult to model, scientists may model only the specific parts of the system they want to study. Their model may be used to show the processes in the system or to make predictions. For example, the system that involves the melting of sea ice in the Arctic is a complex system. **Figure 5** shows how some parts of that system affect each other.

FIGURE 5 ···

How Arctic Sea Ice Melts
The Arctic sea-ice system can be modeled by a diagram.

✎ **Identify** **List some of the variables in the Arctic sea-ice system. Then identify the input, process, and output in this model and fill in the boxes.**

_____

_____

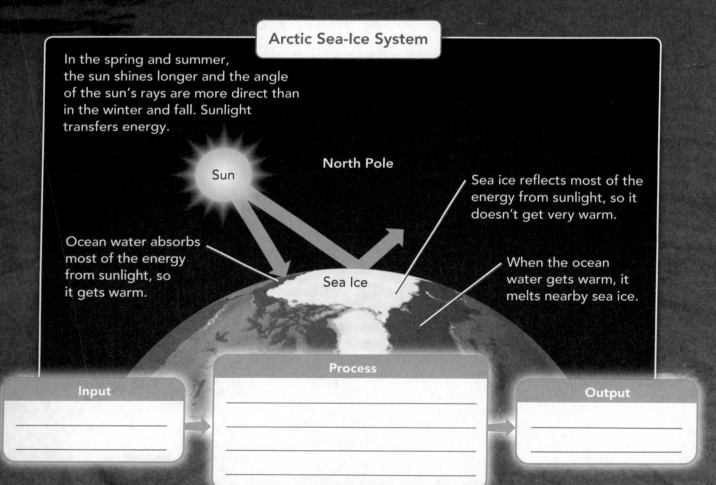

Arctic Sea-Ice System

In the spring and summer, the sun shines longer and the angle of the sun's rays are more direct than in the winter and fall. Sunlight transfers energy.

North Pole

Sun

Sea ice reflects most of the energy from sunlight, so it doesn't get very warm.

Ocean water absorbs most of the energy from sunlight, so it gets warm.

Sea Ice

When the ocean water gets warm, it melts nearby sea ice.

Input

_____

_____

Process

_____

_____

_____

Output

_____

_____

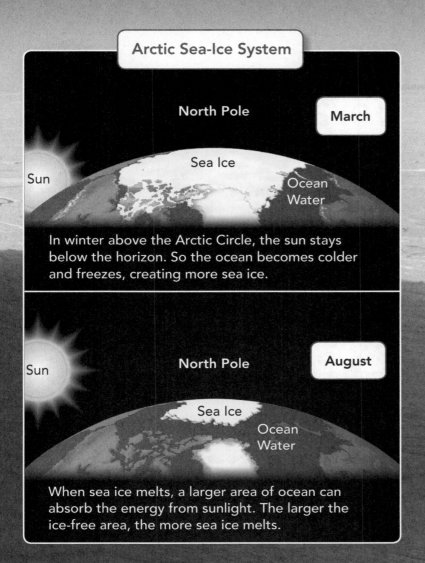

Arctic Sea-Ice System

North Pole — **March**

Sun

Sea Ice

Ocean Water

In winter above the Arctic Circle, the sun stays below the horizon. So the ocean becomes colder and freezes, creating more sea ice.

Sun — **North Pole** — **August**

Sea Ice

Ocean Water

When sea ice melts, a larger area of ocean can absorb the energy from sunlight. The larger the ice-free area, the more sea ice melts.

FIGURE 6 ······························
Arctic Sea-Ice System
These two diagrams show the amount of Arctic sea ice in March and August.

✎ **Answer the questions.**

1. **Describe** In August, what is the feedback in this system?

_____

_____

_____

2. **Explain** What causes changes in the system of melting Arctic sea ice to break the feedback in the system?

_____

_____

_____

Lab zone® Do the Quick Lab *Models in Nature.*

🔑 Assess Your Understanding

2a. Explain Why do scientists use models?

_____

_____

_____

_____

b. Summarize Why aren't models of complex systems completely accurate?

_____

_____

_____

_____

got it? ···

○ **I get it!** Now I know that scientists use models of systems to _____

_____

○ **I need extra help with** _____

Go to **MY SCIENCE COACH** online for help with this subject.

Safety in the Science Laboratory

🔑 Why Prepare for a Laboratory Investigation?

🔑 What Should You Do if an Accident Occurs?

DISASTER

MY PLANET DIARY

Oil Refinery Explosion

On March 23, 2005, an explosion at an oil refinery in Texas took the lives of 15 people and wounded at least 170 others. Sadly, experts agree that this accident could have been prevented had safety codes not been ignored. Investigators found old, worn equipment and noticed that several repairs had not been made. One positive thing that has come out of this accident is a safety video made by the U.S. Chemical Safety Board. The video is based on the refinery accident and includes safety information about how to prevent such an accident from ever occurring again.

Read the following questions. Write your answers below.

1. How do investigators believe this accident might have been prevented?

_____
_____
_____
_____

2. What kind of information would you include in a safety video based on the accident?

_____
_____
_____
_____

> PLANET DIARY Go to **Planet Diary** to learn more about safety in the science laboratory.

Lab zone® Do the Inquiry Warm-Up *Where Is the Safety Equipment in Your School?*

Vocabulary
• safety symbol
• field

Skills
↻ Reading: Summarize
△ Inquiry: Observe

Why Prepare for a Laboratory Investigation?

After hiking for many hours, you reach the campsite. You rush to set up your tent. The tent is lopsided, but it's up, so you run off with your friends. Later that night, heavy rain falls. Water pours into the tent and soaks you. You look for a flashlight. Then you realize that you forgot to pack one. If you had only prepared better, you would be dry and able to see.

Preparing for a Lab Just like for camping, you must prepare before you begin a laboratory investigation, or lab. 🔑 **Good preparation helps you stay safe when doing laboratory investigations.** You should prepare for a lab before you do it. Read through any procedures carefully, and make sure you understand all the directions. If anything is unclear, ask your teacher about it before you begin the lab. Investigations may include safety symbols like the ones you see in **Figure 1. Safety symbols** alert you to possible sources of accidents in a laboratory.

FIGURE 1 ·····················
Safety Symbols
Safety symbols identify how to work carefully and what safety equipment to use.

✎ **Apply Concepts** In the notebook, list symbols that would appear for a lab investigation in which you measure the temperature of water as it heats to boiling.

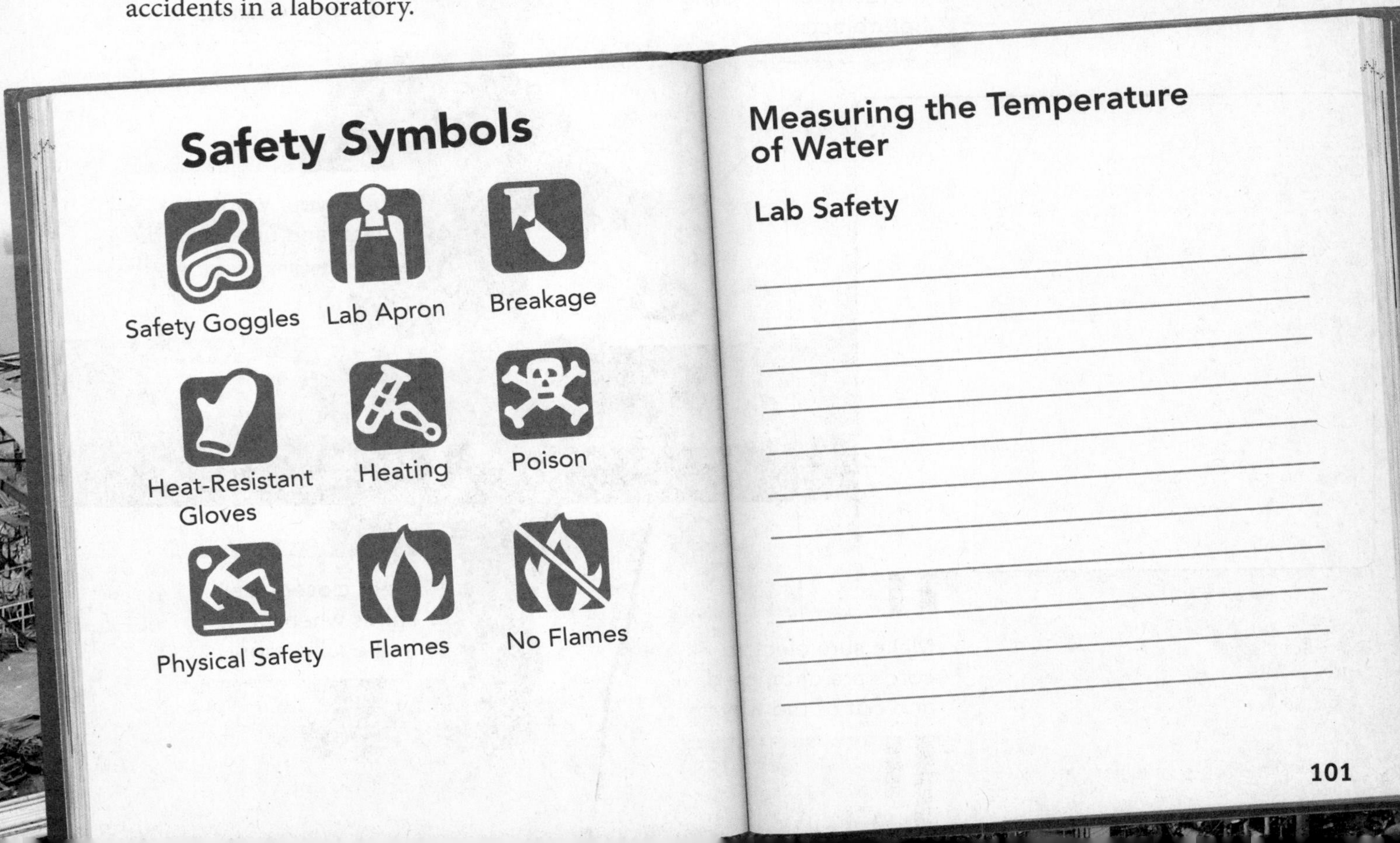

Safety Symbols

 Safety Goggles
 Lab Apron
 Breakage

 Heat-Resistant Gloves
 Heating
 Poison

 Physical Safety
 Flames
 No Flames

Measuring the Temperature of Water

Lab Safety

_____
_____
_____
_____
_____
_____
_____
_____
_____
_____

101

FIGURE 2 ·······························

Safety in the Lab

Recognizing and preventing safety hazards are important skills to practice in the lab.

✎ **Complete the tasks.**

1. **Make Models** In the empty boxes on each page, draw a safety symbol for wearing closed-toe shoes and one for tying back long hair.

2. CHALLENGE How might the student on this page protect himself from breathing in fumes from the flask or beakers?

_____

_____

_____

_____

Performing a Lab

Whenever you do a science lab, your chief concern must be your safety and that of your classmates and your teacher. The most important safety rule is simple: *Always follow your teacher's instructions and the directions exactly.* Never try anything on your own without asking your teacher first.

Figure 2 shows a number of things that you can do to make your lab experience safe and successful. When performing a lab, keep your work area clean and organized. Label all containers so you do not use the wrong chemical accidentally. Also, do not rush through any of the steps. When you need to move around the room, move slowly and carefully so you do not trip or bump into another group's equipment. Finally, always show respect and courtesy to your teacher and classmates.

Wear safety goggles to protect your eyes from chemical splashes, glass breakage, and sharp objects.

Wear an apron to protect yourself and your clothes from chemicals.

Wear heat-resistant gloves when handling hot objects.

Keep your work area clean and uncluttered.

Make sure electric cords are untangled and out of the way.

Wear closed-toe shoes when working in the laboratory.

End-of-Lab Procedures There are important things you need to do at the end of every lab. When you have completed a lab, be sure to clean up your work area. Turn off and unplug any equipment and return it to its proper place. It is very important that you dispose of any waste materials properly. Some wastes should not be thrown in the trash or poured down the drain. Follow your teacher's instructions about proper disposal. Finally, be sure to wash your hands thoroughly after working in the laboratory.

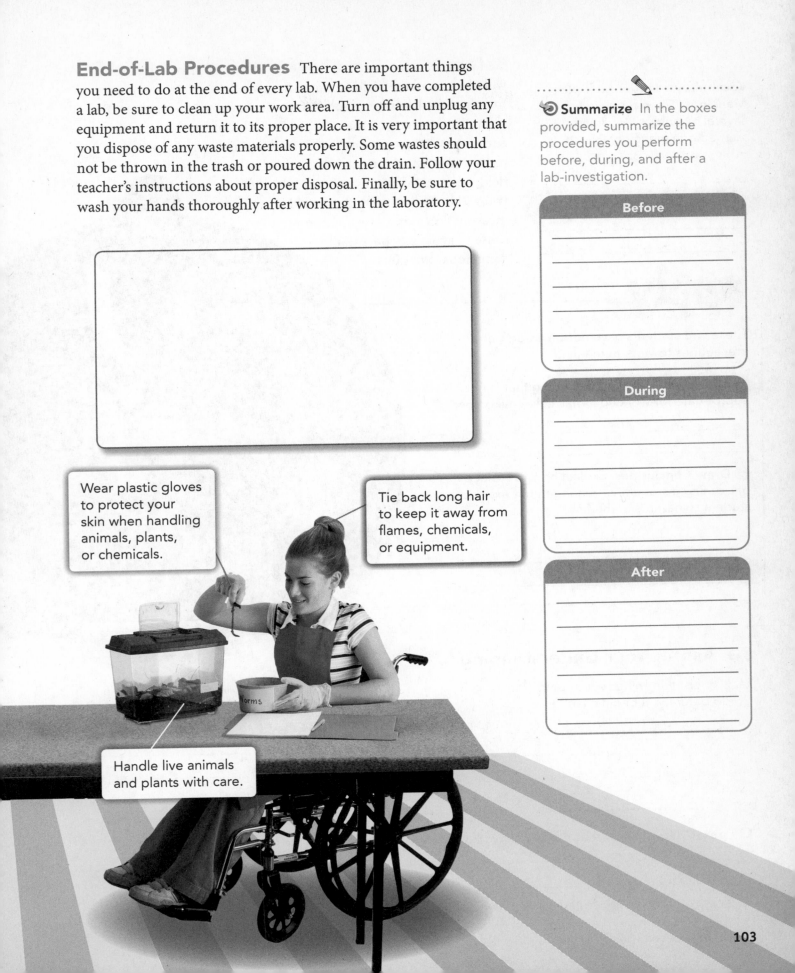

Wear plastic gloves to protect your skin when handling animals, plants, or chemicals.

Tie back long hair to keep it away from flames, chemicals, or equipment.

Handle live animals and plants with care.

🔄 **Summarize** In the boxes provided, summarize the procedures you perform before, during, and after a lab-investigation.

Before

During

After

...........✏.................

Vocabulary Identify Multiple Meanings The noun *field* has several meanings. You have learned one meaning. Give two other meanings for *field*.

_____
_____
_____

Safety in the Field Some of your science investigations will be done in the **field,** or any area outside a science laboratory. Just as in the laboratory, good preparation helps you stay safe. For example, there can be many safety hazards outdoors. You could encounter severe weather, traffic, wild animals, or poisonous plants. Whenever you set out to work in the field, you should always tell an adult where you will be. Never carry out a field investigation alone. Use common sense to avoid any potentially dangerous situations.

apply it!

These two students have not taken proper precautions to work in the field.

1 ▲ **Observe** Identify the clothing that is not appropriate for working in this field environment.

_____
_____

2 Draw Conclusions Explain how one piece of clothing a student is wearing might expose the student to hazards in the field.

_____
_____
_____

Lab zone ® Do the Quick Lab *Be Prepared.*

🗝 Assess Your Understanding

1a. List List two things you should do before you begin a lab.

_____
_____

b. Make Generalizations Why would field investigation take more preparation than a lab investigation?

_____
_____
_____

got it? ....

O **I get it!** Now I know that the key to working safely in the lab and in the field is _____
_____

O **I need extra help with** _____

    Go to MY SCIENCE ⓢ COACH *online for help with this subject.*

What Should You Do if an Accident Occurs?

Although you may have prepared carefully, at some point, an accident may occur. Would you know what to do? You should always start by telling an adult.

🔑 **When any accident occurs, no matter how minor, tell your teacher immediately. Then listen to your teacher's directions and carry them out quickly.** Make sure you know the location and the proper use of all the emergency equipment in your laboratory. Knowing safety and first-aid procedures beforehand will prepare you to handle accidents properly. **Figure 3** lists some emergency procedures.

FIGURE 3 ·············

In Case of Emergency

These first-aid tips can help you in emergency situations in the lab.

✏️ **Read and answer the questions.**

1. **Review** Complete the sentence in the chart to identify the first step in responding to a lab emergency.

2. **Make Judgments** Suppose your teacher is involved in a lab accident. What should you do?

_____

_____

_____

_____

⚠️ **In Case of an Emergency** ⚠️

The first thing to do in an emergency is

_____

Injury	What to Do
Burns	Immerse burns in cold water.
Cuts	Cover cuts with a dressing. Apply direct pressure to stop bleeding.
Spills on Skin	Flush the skin with large amounts of water.
Object in Eye	Flush the eye with water. Seek medical help.

Lab zone® Do the Quick Lab *Just in Case.*

🔑 **Assess Your Understanding**

got it? ···

○ **I get it!** Now I know that the first thing I should do in case of an accident is _____

_____

○ **I need extra help with** _____

Go to **my science COACH** online for help with this subject.

3 Study Guide

Scientists use mathematics to make _____, and to collect, analyze, and display _____.

LESSON 1 Measurement—A Common Language

Using SI as the standard system of measurement allows scientists to compare data and communicate with each other about their results.

In SI, some units of measurement include meter (m), kilogram (kg), cubic meter (m^3), kilograms per cubic meter (kg/m^3), kelvin (K), and second (s).

Vocabulary
• metric system • SI • mass • weight • volume • meniscus • density

LESSON 2 Mathematics and Science

Math skills that scientists use to collect data include estimation, accuracy and precision, and significant figures.

Scientists calculate percent error; find the mean, median, mode, and range; and check reasonableness to analyze data.

Vocabulary
• estimate • accuracy • precision
• significant figures • percent error • mean
• median • mode • range • anomalous data

LESSON 3 Graphs in Science

Line graphs display data that show how the responding variable changes in response to the manipulated variable.

Line graphs are powerful tools in science because they allow you to identify trends, make predictions, and recognize anomalous data.

Vocabulary
• graph • linear graph
• nonlinear graph

LESSON 4 Models as Tools in Science

Models help scientists understand things they cannot observe directly.

A system is a group of parts that work together to produce a specific function or result.

Scientists use models to understand how systems work and to predict how systems might change from feedback or input changes.

Vocabulary
• model • system • input • process
• output • feedback

LESSON 5 Safety in the Science Laboratory

Good preparation helps you stay safe when doing science investigations.

When any accident occurs, no matter how minor, tell your teacher immediately. Then listen to your teacher's directions and carry them out quickly.

Vocabulary
• safety symbol • field

Review and Assessment

LESSON 1 **Measurement— A Common Language**

1. The amount of matter an object contains is its

   a. length.   **b.** mass.

   c. weight.   **d.** volume.

2. The basic SI unit of length is the

_____

3. Measure 0 K is equal to what temperature in Celsius?

_____

4. Compare and Contrast Which of the objects below has a greater volume? Explain.

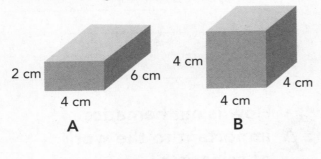

2 cm   6 cm   4 cm   4 cm

4 cm   4 cm

A   **B**

_____

_____

_____

5. Calculate A 12.5 g marble displaces 5.0 mL of water. What is its density?

_____

6. Write About It You are a sports reporter interviewing an Olympic swimmer who lost the silver medal by a few hundredths of a second. Write a one-page interview in which you discuss the meaning of time and the advanced instruments used to measure time.

LESSON 2 **Mathematics and Science**

7. The significant figures in a measurement

   a. include only the first two digits.

   b. include only the estimated digits.

   c. include only the digits that have been measured exactly.

   d. include all of the digits that have been measured exactly, plus one estimated digit.

8. _____ refers to how close a measurement is to the true or accepted value.

9. Apply Concepts What is the median of 7, 31, 86, 6, 20, 85, and 12?

_____

10. Analyze Sources of Error You rush through your lab activity and obtain a percent error of 50 percent. Why might your percent error be so high?

_____

_____

_____

_____

_____

11. do the math! You measure the mass of a mystery object to be 658 g. The actual mass of the object is 755 g. What is your percent error?

LESSON 3 **Graphs in Science**

12. A line graph is used when a manipulated variable is

   a. responsive.   **b.** linear.

   c. continuous.   **d.** anomalous.

13. A _____ is a graph in which the data points do not fall along a straight line.

14. Make Generalizations What do line graphs help you see about your data?

_____

_____

_____

_____

_____

LESSON 4 **Models as Tools in Science**

15. Material or energy that goes into a system is

   a. output.   **b.** input.

   c. feedback.   **d.** process.

16. A _____ system has many parts and variables.

17. Write About It The output of the system below is text displayed on the screen. Describe the input and process that produces this output.

LESSON 5 **Safety in the Science Laboratory**

18. The outdoor area in which some of your scientific investigations will be done is called the

   a. yard.   **b.** lawn.

   c. park.   **d.** field.

19. Good _____ will help you stay safe when performing scientific investigations.

20. Make Judgments Why do you think that you should never bring food into a laboratory?

_____

_____

_____

_____

_____

APPLY THE BIG ❓ **How is mathematics important to the work of scientists?**

21. Civil engineers help plan the construction of buildings. Name three ways the engineers use math during the planning process.

_____

_____

_____

_____

_____

_____

_____

_____

_____

_____

_____

Standardized Test Prep

Multiple Choice

Circle the letter of the best answer.
Use the graph to answer Question 1.

1. What is the general trend in the data?

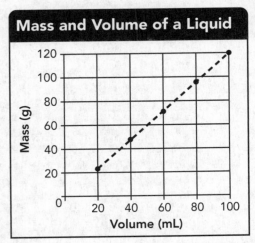

A linear
B no trend
C nonlinear
D linear at first and then nonlinear

2. A student grows tomatoes for an experiment. Which piece of equipment will be needed to determine the mass of the tomato?

A graduated cylinder
B meter stick
C stopwatch
D triple-beam balance

3. Ranida measured a string and got these measurements: 21.5 cm, 21.3 cm, 21.7 cm, and 21.6 cm. The string actually measures 25.5 cm. Which best describes Ranida's measurements?

A They were accurate.
B They were not accurate but they were precise.
C They were both accurate and precise.
D They were neither accurate nor precise.

4. Ellis measured the mass of five samples of quartz. His results were 39.75 g, 38.91 g, 37.66 g, 39.75 g, and 39.55 g. What was the mean mass of the samples?

A 39.55 g
B 39.75 g
C 39.12 g
D 38.91 g

5. Tanya measured an object's mass and volume and calculated its density to be 18 g/cm^3. The object's actual density was 15 g/cm^3. What is Tanya's percent error?

A 17%
B 20%
C 30%
D 83%

Constructed Response

Use the diagram below and your knowledge of science to help you answer Question 6. Write your answer on a separate sheet of paper.

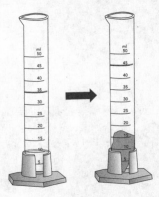

6. Clark decides to measure the volume of a rock he found outside. Based on the diagram above, what method is he using? What is the volume of the rock? Explain your answer.

YOU LOST WHAT?!

Differing measurement systems caused the Mars Climate Orbiter to fly off course and vanish. ▼

In 1999, the National Aeronautics and Space Administration (NASA) made a 125-million-dollar mistake.

That year, the Mars Climate Orbiter was supposed to orbit Mars for one Martian year (687 Earth days). It was to send back information on the planet's atmosphere, surface, and polar caps. Two different teams worked on the orbiter. A team of engineers designed and built it. A team from NASA worked with the engineers to navigate it.

Both teams overlooked a small, but very important detail. The engineering team measured data using Imperial (English) units, while NASA used the metric system. So NASA's navigators assumed that the unit of measurements used to measure how hard the spacecraft's thrusters fired was Newtons per second. Unfortunately, the engineers had programmed the thrusters in pounds per second!

These tiny calculations added up to a big mistake. The spacecraft traveled too close to the surface of Mars and the signal was lost. The 125-million-dollar spacecraft may have been damaged beyond repair when it entered the Martian atmosphere. If not, it bounced off the atmosphere and was lost in space.

Explain It Think of some other examples where a mistake in units could have disastrous results. Write a note to a friend in which you explain why it is always important to include the units with the measurements you are reporting. Include your examples in the note.

Smallpox
on the loose

These days, most people don't worry about contracting smallpox. The last known victim of smallpox died in 1978 and, even then, smallpox was a rare disease. People thought that smallpox was safely contained in labs and that nobody could get sick with it. Then someone did.

Janet Parker was a medical photographer at the University of Birmingham Medical School in England. Scientists working in a lab below her darkroom were researching the smallpox virus. Unfortunately, the laboratory did not have good safety and containment procedures for the deadly virus. Even now, nobody knows exactly how Janet was exposed to the virus, but one theory is that the virus traveled through the air ducts to the darkroom. She became ill and died in September 1978.

Research It The World Health Organization (WHO) declared smallpox completely gone in 1980. What steps did the WHO take to ensure that no one else would contract the disease? In 2002, the WHO decided not to ask the remaining labs to destroy the smallpox stocks. What value do they think the stocks might have? Write a report that answers these questions and include suggestions on what else could or should be done.

WHAT MIGHT THESE TINY ROBOTS DO?

How does technology affect society?

This nanorobot has attached itself to a red blood cell using insectlike legs. Are nanorobots for real? Not yet, but engineers are working to design microscopic robots that may one day be able to perform tasks like injecting medicine into red blood cells.

 Develop Hypotheses What might nanorobots be able to do in the future?

_____

_____

_____

_____

_____

_____

> UNTAMED SCIENCE Watch the **Untamed Science** video to learn more about technology.

Technology and Engineering

4 Getting Started

Check Your Understanding

1. Background Read the paragraph below and then answer the question.

In 1973, Martin Cooper made the first cell phone call from a street in New York City. His **invention** weighed 2.5 pounds! Consider the **impact** of cell phones on everyday life. Cooper's **device** enables people to make and receive calls from nearly anywhere. Callers are no longer tied to wired phones in specific locations.

An **invention** is an original idea, object, or process.

Impact is the effect that something or someone has on the world.

A tool or machine that performs a certain job or function is a **device.**

• How do cell phones impact everyday life?

_____

_____

_____

▶ **MY READING WEB** If you have trouble completing the question above, visit **My Reading Web** and type in *Technology and Engineering.*

Vocabulary Skill

Use Context to Determine Meaning Science books often use unfamiliar words. Look for context clues in surrounding words and phrases to figure out the meaning of *obsolete* in the paragraph below.

A product may become obsolete, or no longer used. For example, typewriters were useful for making written documents. But it was difficult to make changes to the typed document. Today, most people use computers to write and make changes in documents.

Key Term	obsolete
Definition	no longer used
Example	typewriters
Other Information	Today, most people use computers instead.

2. Quick Check Complete the sentence below.

• Typewriters are obsolete, or _____

_____

technology

obsolete

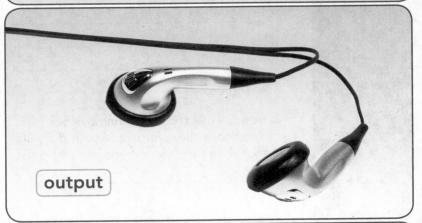

output

risk-benefit analysis

Chapter Preview

LESSON 1
- technology
- engineer
- obsolete
- goal

↻ **Relate Text and Visuals**
△ **Classify**

LESSON 2
- brainstorming
- constraint
- trade-off
- prototype
- troubleshooting
- patent

↻ **Identify the Main Idea**
△ **Communicate**

LESSON 3
- risk-benefit analysis

↻ **Summarize**
△ **Draw Conclusions**

LESSON 4
- engineering
- bioengineering
- aerospace engineering
- mechanical engineering
- civil engineering
- chemical engineering
- electrical engineering

↻ **Relate Cause and Effect**
△ **Infer**

> **VOCAB FLASH CARDS** For extra help with vocabulary, visit **Vocab Flash Cards** and type in *Technology and Engineering.*

UNLOCK THE BIG ?

🔑 What Is the Goal of Technology?

🔑 How Does Technology Progress?

🔑 What Are the Parts of a Technological System?

MY PLANET DIARY

BIOGRAPHY

Lewis H. Latimer (1848–1928) Renaissance Man

You probably know who Thomas Edison and Alexander Graham Bell are. But, do you know who Lewis H. Latimer is? He, too, was an inventor. Latimer was called a "Renaissance man" because he could do many things.

A son of escaped slaves, Latimer enlisted in the Union Navy at the age of 15. After the Civil War ended, Latimer taught himself mechanical drawing. He used the skill to draw the plans for Alexander Graham Bell's invention, the telephone. Later, Latimer took a job at the U.S. Electric Lighting Company, where he invented a different type of electric lamp. He also wrote a groundbreaking book about electric lighting. Not only was Latimer skilled in mechanics, but he was also an artist; he played the flute and wrote plays and poems.

Read the following questions. Write your answers below.

1. What skills did Latimer have that shaped his career?

   Drawing

   _____

   _____

   _____

   _____

2. Besides electric lights, name other inventions that are part of your daily life that didn't exist hundreds of years ago.

   _____

   _____

   _____

▶ PLANET DIARY Go to **Planet Diary** to learn more about understanding technology.

Lab zone® Do the Inquiry Warm-Up *What Are Some Examples of Technology?*

Vocabulary

- technology • engineer • obsolete • goal

Skills

↻ Reading: Relate Text and Visuals

△ Inquiry: Classify

What Is the Goal of Technology?

When you hear the word *technology*, you may think of digital music players and cell phones. As you can see in **Figure 1,** technology includes more than modern devices. Trains and water faucets made life easier for people living in 1900. Ancient inventions, such as stone tools and the wheel, are examples of technology, too.

Meanings of Technology In addition to the devices that people build, technology refers to the knowledge and processes needed to make those things. Put simply, **technology** is the use of knowledge to solve practical problems. ▭ **The goal of technology is to improve the way people live.** For example, eyeglasses improve your ability to see. The Internet allows you to obtain information easily and quickly.

Wheel

To make work easier.

FIGURE 1 ·······································

Technology and You

Technology changes people's lives.

✎ **Infer** Tell how each object has improved the way people live.

Cell phone

Easy to communicate with frieds and family

Washing machine

To wash the laundry easy than to use hands

Areas of Technology Technology can be classified into at least six broad areas: communication, manufacturing, biological and chemical, energy and power, construction, and transportation. The biological and chemical area includes medical technology. Some products of these areas are shown in **Figure 2**.

The six areas of technology are often all involved in improving people's lives. For example, think about the technologies that bring a box of cereal to your table. Trains (transportation) carry grain from a farm to a factory. At the factory (construction), vitamins and minerals (biological and chemical) are added to the grain. The cereal is baked in an oven (energy and power) and then packaged (manufacturing). Trucks transport the boxes to markets, while the cereal is advertised on TV (communication). Finally, you buy the cereal.

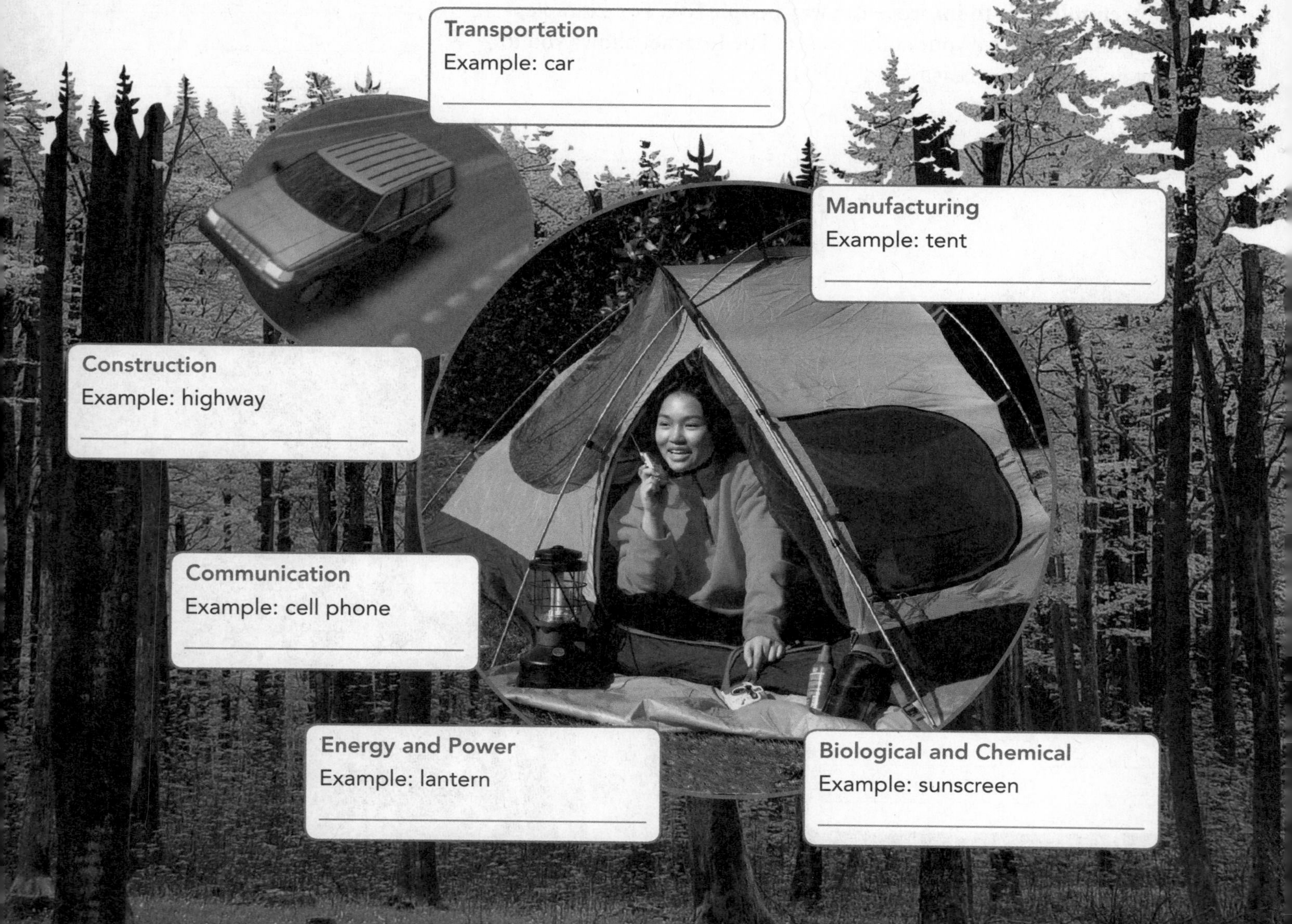

FIGURE 2 ·······································
> INTERACTIVE ART Technology
All Around You
When you go camping, you depend on products from different areas of technology.

✎ Classify In each box, write another example of that technology.

Transportation
Example: car
_____

Manufacturing
Example: tent
_____

Construction
Example: highway
_____

Communication
Example: cell phone
_____

Energy and Power
Example: lantern
_____

Biological and Chemical
Example: sunscreen
_____

1 How light moves through substances was studied.

Science

2 As a result, optical fibers, thin strands of glass or plastic that carry light, were developed.

Technology

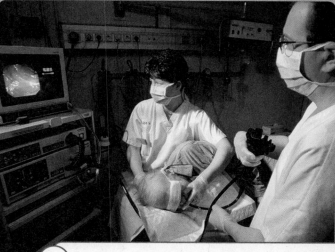

3 Endoscopes use optical fibers to send images. Doctors use endoscopes to view organs within the human body.

Tech + Science

Technology and Science
Although science and technology are different, they often come together to reach a shared goal. Science is the study of the natural world to understand how it functions. People who study the natural world are called scientists. Technology changes the natural world to meet human needs or solve problems. An **engineer** is a person who uses both science and technology to solve problems.

Consider how a scientist and an engineer might view winds. A scientist might study how winds develop and how they affect the weather. An engineer might design a machine that uses wind to produce electricity. Despite these differences, science and technology often depend on each other and affect each other's progress. Look at **Figure 3** to see how science and technology interact.

FIGURE 3 ·······························
Development of the Endoscope
The endoscope is an example of optical fiber technology. Both science and technology contributed to its development.

✎ **Apply Concepts** In each box, indicate whether the description relates to science, technology, or both.

Lab zone® Do the Quick Lab Classifying.

🔑 Assess Your Understanding

1a. Identify What do people use to change the world to meet their needs—science or technology?

_____

_____

b. Communicate How does a telephone fulfill the goal of technology?

_____

_____

got it?

○ **I get it!** Now I know that the goal of technology is _____

_____

○ **I need extra help with** _____

Go to **MY SCIENCE COACH** online for help with this subject.

How Does Technology Progress?

Technology is always changing. Suppose a digital music player you bought six months ago breaks. Chances are good that you will find a more up-to-date system when you shop for a new one. 🔑 **Technology progresses as people's knowledge increases and as new needs can be satisfied.**

Obsolete Technologies Over time, some products may become **obsolete,** or no longer used. For example, typewriters were used to make written documents through the 1980s. They were very noisy, and you could not easily change or save a typed document. With a personal computer, you can make changes easily and save documents. Its user-friendly features helped the personal computer to become popular and to make the typewriter obsolete.

Current Technologies Today, you do not always need a keyboard to type an essay. You can speak it. With voice activation technology, your spoken words appear on your computer screen. But you must speak clearly or the wrong words will appear. Voice activation is a current technology.

✏️ **Relate Text and Visuals**
Identify the advantages and disadvantages of the obsolete and current technologies shown.

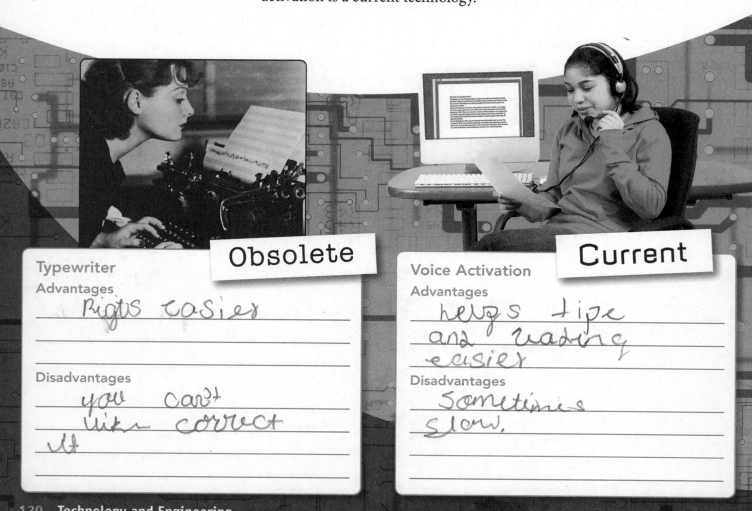

Obsolete

Typewriter

Advantages

Rights easier

Disadvantages

you can't
like correct
it

Current

Voice Activation

Advantages

helps tipe
and reading
easier

Disadvantages

Sometimes
slow.

FIGURE 4 ·······························

An Emerging Technology
A fingertip device that does the work of a computer mouse is an example of an emerging technology.

✏ **Communicate** Talk with a partner about an emerging technology. Name it and list its advantages and disadvantages in the boxes below.

Emerging Technologies Emerging technologies are those that are just beginning to become widely available. For example, the fingertip device shown in **Figure 4** can take the place of a computer mouse. It can interpret your hand movements and communicate them to your computer just as a mouse does. However, emerging technologies may be expensive and may not work perfectly.

Coexisting Technologies Not all old technologies become obsolete. Pens and pencils coexist with current technologies because they still meet people's needs. Also, older, simpler technologies may be more useful than current ones in certain situations. For example, on a camping trip, a hand-operated can opener is more useful than an electric one!

Technology
Jechnoly is a Manmade thing

Advantage
Makes thing easier

Disadvantage
Makes us lary

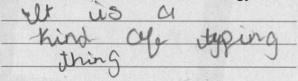
Do the Quick Lab
Processing Words.

🔑 **Assess Your Understanding**

2a. Define What is an obsolete technology?
It is a kind of typing thing

b. Infer Why do you think computer products become obsolete so quickly?
Bayse get spoiled

got it? ···

○ **I get it!** Now I know that technology progresses because _____

○ I need extra help with _____

Go to MY SCIENCE ⑤ COACH *online for help with this subject.*

What Are the Parts of a Technological System?

When you hear the word *system,* what comes to mind? Maybe you think of your school system, or perhaps the solar system. All systems are made of parts that work together. 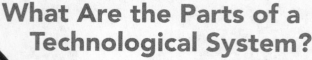 **A technological system includes a goal, inputs, processes, outputs, and in some cases, feedback.**

All technological systems have a particular **goal,** or purpose. An input is something that is put into a system in order to reach that goal. The process is a sequence of actions that the system undergoes as it moves toward that goal. An output is a result or product. If the system works correctly, the output should match the goal. Some technological systems have an additional component called feedback. Feedback is information a system uses to monitor the input, process, and output so that the system can adjust itself to meet the goal. In **Figure 5** you can see a familiar technological system—an oven. An oven is a system that includes feedback.

apply *it!*

A digital music player is an example of a technological system.

❶ Classify Determine which of the descriptions below is the goal, the input, the process, and the output.

a. _____ Push the Play button.

b. _____ The digital file is converted to sound waves.

c. _____ Listen to a song.

d. _____ The player plays the song.

❷ Sequence Write the letter of the steps in the correct order. _____

❸ `CHALLENGE` Name a technological system that you use that includes feedback. _____

FIGURE 5 ....

A System With Feedback

An oven is a technological system with a goal, inputs, processes, outputs, and feedback.

✎ **Evaluate Models and Systems** Read each description. Above each description write the name of the system step it describes.

Input
The gas is turned on.
The temperature is set.
The bread dough is put in.

prosses
Burning gas releases heat. Heat is transferred to air in the oven. The temperature increases.

output
The bread bakes.

Feedback
A thermostat monitors temperature. If the temperature falls below the set level, then the gas flow is turned on. If the temperature increases above the set level, then the gas flow shuts off.

goal
To bake a loaf of whole wheat bread.

Lab zone Do the Lab Investigation *Investigating a Technological System.*

🗝 Assess Your Understanding

3a. Review How does a technological system adjust itself?

It was made to adjust itself.

b. Apply Concepts An alarm clock is a technological system. Identify the output.

you have to ge

got it?

○ **I get it!** Now I know that the components of a technological system are _____

_____

_____

○ **I need extra help with** _____

Go to MY SCIENCE ⓢ COACH *online for help with this subject.*

Technological Design

UNLOCK THE BIG ? What Are the Technology Design Steps?

MY PLANET DIARY

A Sticky Problem

Art Fry was frustrated. The bits of paper that he used to mark his place in his church hymnal kept falling out. He remembered that Spencer Silver, another scientist at the company where he worked, was developing an adhesive. Silver was not happy with the adhesive because it was weaker than what he wanted. But, it was just strong enough to hold pieces of paper together and still allow users to pull them apart again. Fry used some of the adhesive to coat his bits of paper. After a number of years of development, Fry and Silver had invented sticky notes!

Do the Inquiry Warm-Up Why Redesign?

DISCOVERY

Answer the questions below.

1. Use Art Fry's experience to explain the phrase "necessity is the mother of invention."

_____

_____

_____

2. Why is communication between engineers important?

_____

_____

_____

> PLANET DIARY Go to **Planet Diary** to learn more about technological design.

What Are the Technology Design Steps?

If you had used a computer 60 years ago, you would not have used a mouse. The mouse was the result of a technology design process to translate the motion of your hand into signals the computer can read. **The steps for designing technology include identifying a need, researching the problem, designing a solution, building a prototype, troubleshooting and redesigning, and communicating the solution.**

Vocabulary
- brainstorming
- constraint
- trade-off
- prototype
- troubleshooting
- patent

Skills
- Reading: Identify the Main Idea
- Inquiry: Communicate

Identify a Need The mouse was originally designed so people did not have to use the arrow buttons on a keyboard to move the cursor on the screen. Early versions were expensive. They also had several problems. Dirt became trapped inside, preventing the devices from working. They often "slipped." That is, the cursor didn't move when the mouse was moved. To improve the original mouse, the engineer in **Figure 1** first had to decide what need he was trying to meet. To identify a need, engineers clearly define the problem they are trying to solve. The overall need that the engineering team identified was for a non-slipping mouse that would be easy to use. They wanted the device to be inexpensive, safe, and to last a long time.

Identify a Need

My cursor won't move! This mouse slips all the time.

FIGURE 1 ....
Identifying Needs
This engineer is having trouble with his mouse.

✎ **Identify a Need** On the notebook paper, write why the mouse was redesigned.

Research the Problem After defining a problem, engineers research it by gathering information that will help them solve the problem. There are many ways that engineers research information about a new product, as shown in **Figure 2.** They may read books and articles. They may also attend conferences and share ideas with others. Engineers usually perform experiments to test the technology. In addition, they may talk to people like you to find out what customers want.

To gather information about the mouse, the engineers conducted many tests. They knew that the ball inside the mouse was held in place by a complex system of sensitive, costly parts. Because the parts were so sensitive, they found that too much pressure on the ball made it slip. In addition, any bit of dirt or dust would jam the system. This problem caused the mouse to stop working about once a week. To fix it, the entire mouse had to be taken apart, and each part had to be cleaned separately.

FIGURE 2 ·····································

Researching
Research is an important step in the design process.

✎ **Research the Problem** On the notebook page, write three things discovered during the research for the original mouse.

Design a Solution Designing a solution involves coming up with ideas that address the problem. The best design meets the needs and has the fewest negative characteristics.

Generate Ideas Have you and your friends ever met to come up with ideas for a special event? **Brainstorming** is a process in which group members suggest any solutions that come to mind. Many ideas are better than only a few ideas because you don't know which idea might work. After brainstorming, engineers may sketch or model their ideas. **Figure 3** shows these steps.

Identify Materials For physical products, engineers must consider the strength and performance of the materials they use. For example, the parts of a mouse must stand up to repeated use and resist breaking. Materials also must be safe to use.

FIGURE 3 ··
Designing a Solution
Designing a solution takes multiple steps.

✎ **Design a Solution** Label each picture with the design process step it illustrates. On the notebook paper, list the engineers' brainstorming ideas.

Watch ideas take off as you model some stages of the design process.

❶ Communicate With three or four classmates, brainstorm some ideas for a new product that gets all of the peanut butter out of a container.

_____

_____

_____

_____

_____

❷ Work with Design Constraints Evaluate each idea, and discuss the constraints and trade-offs you might have to make.

_____

_____

_____

_____

_____

_____

_____

_____

❸ Design a Solution Sketch the design solution the team has agreed on.

Evaluate Constraints In **Figure 4** you can see the result of a mouse with a ball that creates too much friction. Friction is the force produced when two surfaces rub against each other. If the ball inside a mouse is made of a material with too much "grip," it will not move. The material and the friction it produces are constraints. A **constraint** is any factor that limits a design.

Make Trade-Offs One material may be sturdy but look ugly. Another material may be attractive but not strong. The design team may decide to use the more attractive material, which will appeal to customers. In this case, the team would be trading off strength for appearance. A **trade-off** is an exchange in which one benefit is given up in order to obtain another.

FIGURE 4 ⋯⋯⋯⋯⋯⋯⋯⋯⋯⋯⋯⋯⋯⋯⋯⋯

The Mouse Design Process Continues

Solving problems and making choices are part of designing a new product.

✎ **Identify** Label each picture with the appropriate design process step.

Build a Prototype After considering constraints and trade-offs, engineers build and test a prototype. A **prototype** is a working model used to test a design. Some prototypes may be full-size and made of the materials proposed for the final product. Others are completely virtual, or computer generated.

Prototypes are used to test the operation of a product. Prototypes test how well the product works, how long it lasts, and how safe it is to use. A design team may have some people use the prototype and evaluate it. Engineers may also test the prototype in a lab to see how it works, as shown in **Figure 5.** Or, they may use computers to test virtual models. Test results help determine how well the product meets the goals and what improvements are still needed.

FIGURE 5 ···

Using Prototypes

Prototypes show how well a design works.

✎ **Build a Prototype** Label each picture with the appropriate design step. On the notebook paper, describe the best way to test a prototype of a mouse. Explain why this method works.

129

FIGURE 6 ··························
▶ INTERACTIVE ART

Troubleshooting and Redesigning

✎ These engineers are troubleshooting and working on a redesign.

1. **Label** In the boxes, write down the design process step each picture shows.

2. **Troubleshoot** Write in the table the problems with the mouse that caused the optical mouse to be invented.

3. CHALLENGE Why is it wise to provide time and money to redesign a product?

_____

_____

_____

_____

Troubleshoot	Redesign

Troubleshoot and Redesign

Prototype tests may uncover design problems. For example, tests may show that people have difficulty using a product or that a part breaks easily. The causes of any problems must be identified and the product must be redesigned. The process of analyzing a design problem and finding a way to fix it is called **troubleshooting**.

In **Figure 6,** you can see a problem with the mouse that prototype tests revealed. The mouse was noisy. Troubleshooting identified the rolling ball as the cause of the noise. The engineers replaced the steel ball with a rubber ball to make the mouse quieter. Engineers also added an easy-to-open ring-shaped cap. This redesign also made the mouse easy to clean.

Mouse technology progressed even further after these problems were solved. A wireless optical mouse uses a laser instead of a ball and can have a sensor instead of a wire connected to the computer.

Communicate the Solution

Communicate the Solution

I need a mouse.

I need three mouses.

Don't you mean three mice?

EVERYBODY NEEDS A MOUSE

U.S. Patent Office

FIGURE 7 ·····················
Communicating the Solution
Communicating about a new technology shows customers the new product.

✏ **List** Write the ways communication occurs in the picture.

_____

_____

Communicate the Solution The last stage of the technology design process is communicating the solution. Engineers must explain the design to manufacturers who will produce the product. The engineers must describe their product to advertisers. In doing so, they must also communicate how a product meets the consumer's needs. Look at **Figure 7** to see some ways that engineers communicate.

Frequently, inventors or companies will obtain patents to protect their inventions. A **patent** is a legal document issued by a government that gives the inventor exclusive rights to make, use, or sell the invention over a certain period of time. If others want to use the invention, they must obtain the patent owner's permission and pay a fee. After the patent's time runs out, however, anyone can make or sell the invention.

·····················✏·····················
🔁 **Identify the Main Idea**
Circle the main idea in the first paragraph. Underline the details.

Lab zone® Do the Quick Lab *Watch Ideas Take Off.*

⛋ Assess Your Understanding

1a. Explain What are design constraints?

_____

_____

b. Infer What steps would engineers take if there are problems with optical mice?

_____

_____

got it? ·····················

○ I get it! Now I know that technology design steps are to: _____

_____

_____

○ I need extra help with _____

Go to MY SCIENCE 🔵 COACH *online for help with this subject.*

Technology and Society

- How Has Technology Impacted Society?

- What Are the Consequences of Technology?

- How Do You Decide Whether to Use a Technology?

MY PLANET DIARY   FUN FACTS

A Super-Duper Sponge

Imagine a material that can hold 100 times its own weight in water. Superabsorbents can do just that. They start as powdery pellets. Then as the pellet absorbs water, it swells and turns into a rubbery gel.

Superabsorbent material is used in a variety of ways. For example, it has replaced the cotton and paper wadding in baby diapers. Also, superabsorbents are used in meat packaging to prevent leaks.

Read the following question. Write your answer below.

What are two other possible uses for superabsorbent material?

_____

_____

_____

_____

_____

> PLANET DIARY Go to **Planet Diary** to learn more about technology and society.

Lab zone® Do the Inquiry Warm-Up *Technology Hunt.*

How Has Technology Impacted Society?

In the early 1800s, skilled weavers lost their jobs as textile factories started to use a new technology—looms run by steam power. Job loss is one example of how technology affects society. However, technology can also create jobs because workers are needed to build new machines and tools. **From the Stone Age thousands of years ago to the Information Age today, technology has had a large impact on society.**

Vocabulary
• risk-benefit analysis

Skills
↻ Reading: Summarize
△ Inquiry: Draw Conclusions

Stone Age and Iron Age   During the Stone Age, people used stones to make tools. Spears, axes, and spades enabled people to hunt and grow crops. As the food supply became more stable, people did not have to wander as far to find food. As a result, they began to settle into farming communities. During the Iron Age, people produced iron and used it to make tools. Machines, such as plows, were improved. Plows enabled farmers to grow more food.

Industrial Revolution   The Industrial Revolution brought about steam- and water-powered machines that replaced smaller human-powered machines. These new machines introduced the mass production of many goods.

Information Age   Today, in the Information Age, satellites, cell phones, and computers allow people to share information quickly. Distant societies no longer have to be isolated from one another.

Steam-Powered Spinning Machine

Modern Loom

FIGURE 1 ···

Mass Production
A steam-powered spinning machine could produce many spools of thread at one time. A modern loom can weave the material for one shirt in less than a minute.

✎ **Analyze Costs and Benefits** What is one cost and one benefit of the modern loom?

_____

_____

_____

_____

Do the Quick Lab
Time-Saving Technology.

━━ **Assess Your Understanding**

got it? ···

○ **I get it!** Now I know that since the Stone Age, technology has _____

_____

○ **I need extra help with** _____

Go to MY SCIENCE ⑤ COACH *online for help with this subject.*

What Are the Consequences of Technology?

Technological advances have done much to move societies forward. However, technology has other consequences. 🔑 **In addition to intended consequences, a technology can have unintended consequences on society and the environment.**

The Environment Many technologies, such as dams and pesticides, affect the environment. For example, pesticides protect crops from insects. This technology allows farmers to grow more crops. More crops means food prices stay low, which was an intended consequence. However, rain can wash pesticides into rivers and water supplies. The pesticides can then affect plants and animals that live in the water and people who use the water supply. This was an unintended consequence.

Jobs Technology increases the amount of work people can do in the same amount of time. For example, farmers can plow more land with a tractor than with a horse-drawn plow. Therefore, farms with tractors require fewer workers. In the 1900s, this led to an unintended consequence: many people lost their jobs.

do the math!

Working on the Farm

The graph shows the percentage of workers on farms between the years 1860 and 2000. Use the graph to answer the following questions.

1 Interpret Data In which year was the percentage of farm workers the highest? In which year was the percentage the lowest?

_____

2 Calculate By how much did the percentage of farm workers change between 1860 and 2000?

_____

3 ◢Draw Conclusions What trend does the graph show?

_____

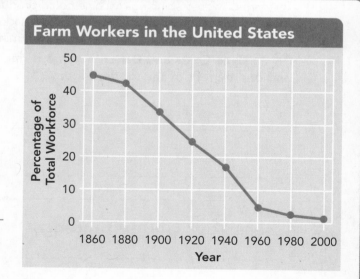

Farm Workers in the United States

Percentage of Total Workforce vs. Year (1860–2000)

Health and Safety One intended consequence of technology products is to help people live long, healthy lives. For example, air bags have saved many lives. However, they also have unintended consequences. The explosive force of inflating airbags has injured and killed people, especially small children. The hot gases in an air bag can also cause serious burns.

Energy Technology has made more energy available for use. For example, refineries change crude oil into the gasoline that fuels cars. Power plants have the intended consequence of generating electricity that lights millions of homes. But power plants and cars have the unintended consequence of causing air pollution.

Pace of Life Technological advances enable people to do things more quickly today. Frozen foods help you prepare meals in minutes. Computers help workers do more tasks in a shorter time. However, being able to do things quickly may make some people feel rushed to get more things done. Use **Figure 2** to identify the consequences on society of using horses and buggies and cars.

did you
know?
In 1946, Percy Spencer was working on a device that produced microwave radio signals. He was standing near it when the chocolate bar in his pocket melted. Spencer figured out it was the microwaves. To test it further, Spencer placed a bag of popcorn kernels next to the device. The kernels popped and he had cooked popcorn. Percy's accidental discovery gave society the microwave oven.

FIGURE 2 ··

Modes of Transportation

✎ **Communicate** Work with a partner to describe the consequences on society of using horses and buggies and cars.

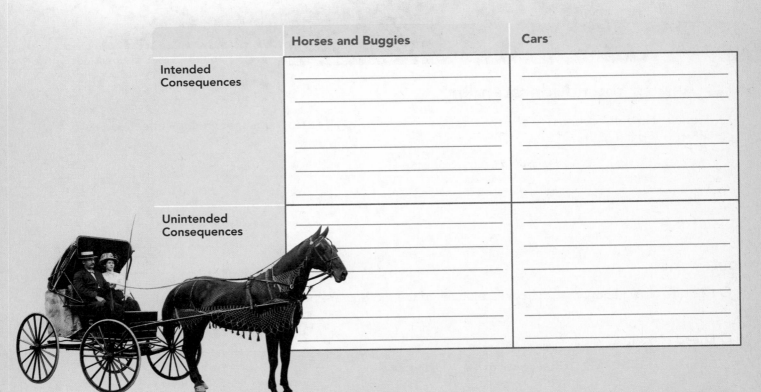

	Horses and Buggies	Cars
Intended Consequences		
Unintended Consequences		

A Computerized Society

How does technology affect society?

FIGURE 3 ....

>ART IN MOTION Computers affect society in many ways.

✎ **Evaluate the Impact on Society** Circle two choices from the word bank, and write examples of how computers have affected society for each of your choices.

Word Bank
The Environment
Jobs
Health and Safety
Energy
Pace of Life

My choice:

_____
_____
_____
_____
_____
_____

My choice:

_____
_____
_____
_____
_____
_____

Lab zone® Do the Quick Lab *How Does Technology Affect Your Life?*

🔑 Assess Your Understanding

1a. Explain How do technological advances affect our pace of life?

_____
_____
_____
_____

b. **ANSWER THE BIG ?** How does technology affect society?

_____
_____
_____
_____

got it? ....

○ **I get it!** Now I know that the consequences of technology are both _____
_____

○ **I need extra help with** _____

Go to **MY SCIENCE COACH** online for help with this subject.

How Do You Decide Whether to Use a Technology?

If a technology can have unintended consequences, then how can people decide whether or not to use it? 🔧 **In deciding whether to use a technology, people must analyze its possible risks and benefits.** Risk-benefit analysis involves evaluating the possible problems, or risks, of a technology compared to the expected advantages, or benefits. People often reach different conclusions about risks and benefits.

Identifying Risks and Benefits Suppose a company makes a new bicycle helmet out of a light-weight material. The helmet provides less protection than heavier helmets, but it is more comfortable. A government agency finds that the main risk of the new helmet is the greater possibility of injury than with heavier helmets. But, riders find heavier helmets uncomfortable and may avoid wearing them. The benefit of the new helmet is that more people would have some form of head protection, rather than no protection at all. Should you use the new helmet?

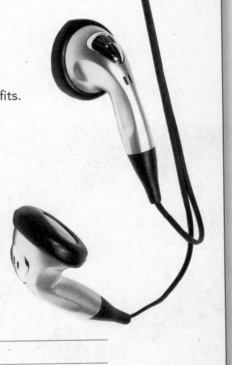

apply it!

Earbud headphones have risks and benefits.

1 ▷ **Draw Conclusions** Decide if each item below is a risk or a benefit of using these headphones. Write *R* next to the risks and *B* next to the benefits.

- _____ Can tune out loud noises in the environment
- _____ Can damage hearing at high volumes
- _____ Can let you listen to your own music without disturbing others
- _____ Can be lost easily
- _____ Can prevent you from hearing oncoming traffic
- _____ Can be carried easily

2 **Analyze Costs and Benefits** Based on your risk-benefit analysis, should you use headphones? Why or why not?

_____

_____

_____

Values and Trade-Offs

Often in evaluating a technology's risks and benefits, human values must be considered. A value is something that is important to a person or society. Values might be health, honesty, and personal freedom.

Difficulties can arise when one value favors a technology while another value cautions against it. In the case of new helmets, the conflicting values could be safety versus people's comfort. When values conflict, a decision involves trade-offs. A trade-off consists of exchanging one benefit for another. For example, by choosing the lightweight helmet, people trade their safety for comfort.

Other trade-offs may involve conflict between economic and environmental values. For example, continuing to use current power plants may be less expensive than developing new power plants. However, the new plants could cause less pollution. **Figure 4** shows examples of technologies that involve trade-offs.

Vocabulary Use Context to Determine Meaning Underline the context clues that help you understand the meaning of *trade-off*. Circle the additional details that show its meaning.

FIGURE 4 ·······································

Trade-offs

Coal plants use coal to produce energy. Wind farms use wind to produce energy.

✎ **Analyze Costs and Benefits** What are some trade-offs of coal plants and wind farms? Write your answers in the table.

	Trade-offs
Coal Plants	
Wind Farms	

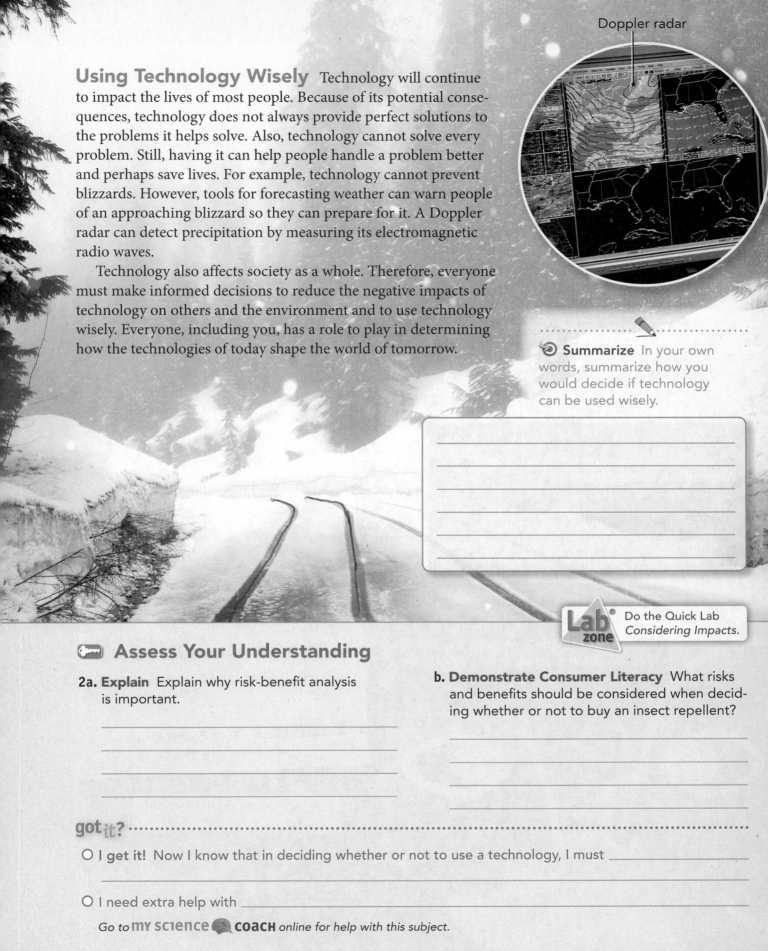

Doppler radar

Using Technology Wisely Technology will continue to impact the lives of most people. Because of its potential consequences, technology does not always provide perfect solutions to the problems it helps solve. Also, technology cannot solve every problem. Still, having it can help people handle a problem better and perhaps save lives. For example, technology cannot prevent blizzards. However, tools for forecasting weather can warn people of an approaching blizzard so they can prepare for it. A Doppler radar can detect precipitation by measuring its electromagnetic radio waves.

Technology also affects society as a whole. Therefore, everyone must make informed decisions to reduce the negative impacts of technology on others and the environment and to use technology wisely. Everyone, including you, has a role to play in determining how the technologies of today shape the world of tomorrow.

⊙ **Summarize** In your own words, summarize how you would decide if technology can be used wisely.

Lab zone® Do the Quick Lab *Considering Impacts.*

⚷ Assess Your Understanding

2a. Explain Explain why risk-benefit analysis is important.

b. Demonstrate Consumer Literacy What risks and benefits should be considered when deciding whether or not to buy an insect repellent?

got it? ....

○ **I get it!** Now I know that in deciding whether or not to use a technology, I must _____

○ I need extra help with _____

Go to MY SCIENCE ⓢ COACH *online for help with this subject.*

LESSON
4 Engineering

UNLOCK THE BIG ?

🔑 **What Is Engineering?**

🔑 **What Are Some Branches of Engineering?**

🔑 **How Does Engineering Benefit Society?**

MY PLANET DiARY

Posted by: Aaliyah

Location: Brewerton, New York

One modern invention has helped me throughout my entire life—my hearing aids. They come with an FM system and they help me hear people. This invention helps me at school so I can listen in class and at home so I can hear the TV. The FM system acts just like a microphone, but instead of everyone hearing the sound it only goes into my hearing aids. If I didn't have my hearing aids, my life would be completely different. I wouldn't be able to socialize and I would be so lonely without any friends. This invention has helped me my entire life and it is really worth it!

BLOG

Read the following questions. Write your answers below.

1. How are Aaliyah's hearing aids similar to a microphone? How are they different?

_____
_____
_____
_____
_____
_____
_____

2. What is one modern invention that has helped you? How has it helped?

_____
_____
_____

 PLANET DIARY Go to **Planet Diary** to learn more about engineering.

 Do the Inquiry Warm-Up *What Is Engineering?*

Vocabulary

- engineering • bioengineering • aerospace engineering
- mechanical engineering • civil engineering
- chemical engineering • electrical engineering

Skills

↻ Reading: Relate Cause and Effect

△ Inquiry: Infer

What Is Engineering?

Think about all the things you do to get ready for school. You get dressed, eat breakfast, and brush your teeth. The zipper on your pants, the microwave that cooked your cereal, even your toothpaste tube are examples of products designed by engineering. **Engineering** is the application of science to satisfy needs and solve problems. ⊙ **Engineering requires both scientific and technical knowledge to design things that make life better.**

apply it!

Look at the photos of products designed to make people's lives easier.

❶ ↻ **Relate Cause and Effect** Label each picture with the letter of the problem the product was designed to solve.

A. Prevent people from getting wet

B. Allow travel over difficult terrain

C. Make food last longer

D. Perform difficult math calculations

❷ CHALLENGE Name an unintended consequence of a refrigerator.

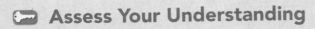

Lab zone® Do the Quick Lab *Designing a Solution.*

⊙ Assess Your Understanding

got it?

○ I get it! Now I know that engineering requires both _____

_____

○ I need extra help with _____

Go to **my science COACH** *online for help with this subject.*

FIGURE 1

> REAL-WORLD INQUIRY **Branches of Engineering**

There are many different branches of engineering.

✎ **Identify** Read each description. Name another product that was developed by each branch of engineering. You can use the Internet to find examples.

Bioengineering involves applying engineering principles to biology and medicine to create processes and products such as artificial limbs and X-ray machines.

_____

_____

Aerospace engineering consists of the design, construction, and testing of airplanes and spacecraft.

_____

_____

What Are Some Branches of Engineering?

People from many areas of engineering may be involved in the development of an engineering product. For example, it takes the work of many engineers to get a space shuttle off the ground. Some engineers determine a space shuttle's shape and design. They also calculate the thrust needed to lift the space shuttle. Other engineers find the best fuel mixtures for the space shuttle engines.

🔑 **Engineering has many branches.** They include bioengineering, aerospace engineering, mechanical engineering, civil engineering, chemical engineering, and electrical engineering. Some of the common branches of engineering are

Mechanical engineering deals with the design, construction, and operation of machinery such as cars or personal transporters.

_____

_____

Civil engineering includes the design and construction of roads, bridges, and buildings.

_____

This is a personal transporter.

Chemical engineering deals with the conversion of chemicals, such as oil, into useful products, such as diesel fuel.

_____

_____

Electrical engineering involves the design of electrical systems, including power, control systems, and telecommunications, such as satellites.

_____

_____

 Lab zone ® Do the Quick Lab _Branches of Engineering._

🔑 Assess Your Understanding

1a. ⚠️ **Infer** Why do you think there are many types of engineering?

_____

_____

_____

b. Classify What branches of engineering were involved in making a hair dryer?

_____

_____

_____

got it?

○ **I get it!** Now I know that the branches of engineering include _____

_____

_____

_____

_____

_____

○ **I need extra help with** _____

_Go to_ **my science** 🔵 **COACH** _online for help with this subject._

How Does Engineering Benefit Society?

What would life be like without electricity? You could not use the Internet, play video games, or recharge your digital music player. However, usually you do have electricity every day because of power lines and generators designed by engineers. 🔑 **Engineers design products that improve our daily lives in many ways, including saving lives, energy, and time and effort.**

Saving Lives In 2004, a tsunami (tsoo NAH mee), or giant ocean wave, washed over southeast Asia. It was one of the worst natural disasters ever—more than one million people lost their homes. As a result, engineers designed a tsunami early-warning system in the Indian Ocean, as shown in **Figure 2**. The early-warning system gives people in high-risk areas time to reach safe ground.

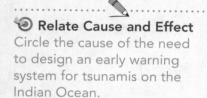

Relate Cause and Effect
Circle the cause of the need to design an early warning system for tsunamis on the Indian Ocean.

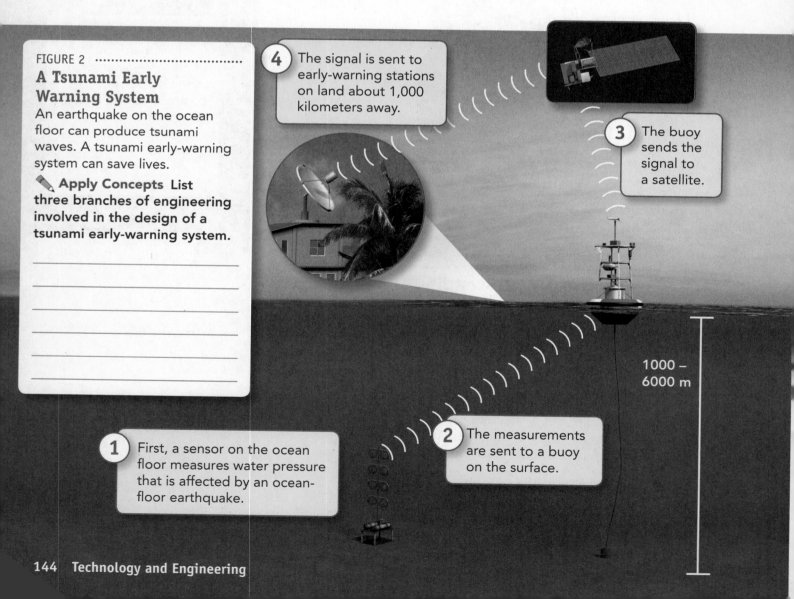

FIGURE 2 ⋯⋯⋯⋯⋯⋯⋯⋯

A Tsunami Early Warning System

An earthquake on the ocean floor can produce tsunami waves. A tsunami early-warning system can save lives.

✎ **Apply Concepts** List three branches of engineering involved in the design of a tsunami early-warning system.

_____

_____

_____

_____

_____

_____

4 The signal is sent to early-warning stations on land about 1,000 kilometers away.

3 The buoy sends the signal to a satellite.

1 First, a sensor on the ocean floor measures water pressure that is affected by an ocean-floor earthquake.

2 The measurements are sent to a buoy on the surface.

1000 – 6000 m

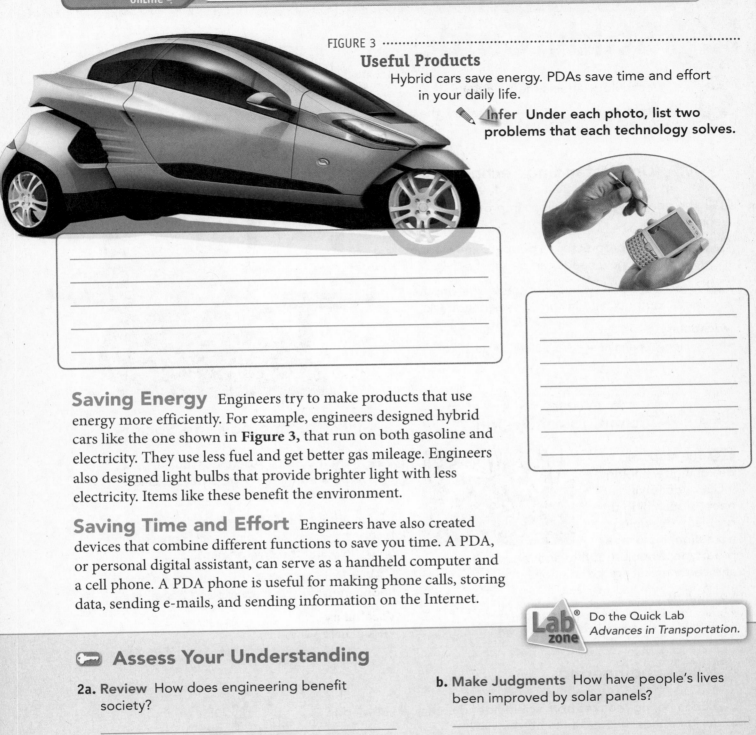

FIGURE 3 ··································

Useful Products

Hybrid cars save energy. PDAs save time and effort in your daily life.

✐ **Infer** Under each photo, list two problems that each technology solves.

Saving Energy

Engineers try to make products that use energy more efficiently. For example, engineers designed hybrid cars like the one shown in **Figure 3,** that run on both gasoline and electricity. They use less fuel and get better gas mileage. Engineers also designed light bulbs that provide brighter light with less electricity. Items like these benefit the environment.

Saving Time and Effort

Engineers have also created devices that combine different functions to save you time. A PDA, or personal digital assistant, can serve as a handheld computer and a cell phone. A PDA phone is useful for making phone calls, storing data, sending e-mails, and sending information on the Internet.

Lab zone® Do the Quick Lab *Advances in Transportation.*

🔑 Assess Your Understanding

2a. Review How does engineering benefit society?

_____

_____

_____

b. Make Judgments How have people's lives been improved by solar panels?

_____

_____

_____

got it? ··································

○ **I get it!** Now I know that engineering benefits society by _____

_____

○ I need extra help with _____

Go to **MY SCIENCE COACH** online for help with this subject.

Study Guide

Technology affects the _____, the number of _____ and how they are performed, _____ and safety, the amount of _____ used, and the _____ of life.

LESSON 1 Understanding Technology

🔑 The goal of technology is to improve the way people live.

🔑 Technology progresses as people's knowledge increases and as new needs can be satisfied.

🔑 A technological system includes a goal, inputs, processes, outputs, and in some cases, feedback.

Vocabulary
• technology • engineer • obsolete • goal

LESSON 2 Technological Design

🔑 The steps for designing technology include identifying a need, researching the problem, designing a solution, building a prototype, troubleshooting and redesigning, and communicating the solution.

Vocabulary
• brainstorming • constraint • trade-off
• prototype • troubleshooting • patent

LESSON 3 Technology and Society

🔑 From the Stone Age thousands of years ago to the Information Age today, technology has had a large impact on society.

🔑 In addition to intended consequences, a technology can have unintended consequences on society and the environment.

🔑 In deciding whether to use a technology, people must analyze its risks and benefits.

Vocabulary
• risk-benefit analysis

LESSON 4 Engineering

🔑 Engineering requires both scientific and technical knowledge to design things that make life better.

🔑 Engineering has many branches. They include bioengineering, aerospace engineering, mechanical engineering, civil engineering, chemical engineering, and electrical engineering.

🔑 Engineers design and build products that improve our daily lives in many ways, including saving lives, energy, time, and effort.

Vocabulary
• engineering • bioengineering • aerospace engineering • mechanical engineering
• civil engineering • chemical engineering • electrical engineering

Review and Assessment

LESSON 1 **Understanding Technology**

1. The goal of technology is to

   a. use resources irresponsibly.

   b. improve the way people live.

   c. design flashier products.

   d. design smaller products.

2. A well-designed technological system will have an output that matches its _____

3. Compare and Contrast Give an example of an obsolete technology and a coexisting technology.

_____

_____

_____

_____

_____

4. Classify For the system shown below, identify the input, process, and output.

Car moves forward. | Driver steps on the gas pedal. | Gas makes the engine run.

(_____) (_____) (_____)

5. **Write About It** Choose a current technological product, such as a calculator, with which you are familiar. Suppose that you are a news reporter. Write a brief report that covers the product's first introduction to the public.

LESSON 2 **Technological Design**

6. To design a cell phone, engineers consider how its size and sound reception may limit its design. What are these factors called?

   a. prototypes   **b.** patents

   c. trade-offs   **d.** constraints

7. When engineers _____, they may read books to gather information.

8. Sequence What will an engineer do after designing a solution?

_____

_____

_____

9. Relate Cause and Effect How do patents help reward creativity?

_____

_____

_____

_____

_____

10. Make Judgments A team working on a new bicycle seat design must choose between a comfortable but costly design and an uncomfortable but less expensive design. Which trade-off would you make? Explain.

_____

_____

_____

_____

_____

_____

CHAPTER
4

LESSON 3 Technology and Society

11. The process of evaluating possible problems with a technology, as well as its expected advantages, is called

    a. feedback.   **b.** risk-benefit analysis.

    c. brainstorming.   **d.** prototyping.

12. A new technology can have both _____ _____ consequences on society and the environment.

Use the table below to answer Question 13.

Number of Trains in Use in the United States, 1900 and 1960		
Type	1900	1960
Steam trains	37,463	374
Electric trains	200	498
Diesel trains	0	30,240

13. Interpret Data What type of train met people's needs best in 1960? Explain.

_____

_____

_____

_____

14. Analyze Costs and Benefits Describe a risk and a benefit of traveling by airplane.

_____

_____

_____

_____

15. Write About It Suppose you are organizing an exhibit at a museum featuring inventions that have impacted society. Choose one invention. Write a summary about the invention to be posted at the exhibit.

LESSON 4 Engineering

16. An artificial arm is an example of a product designed by

    a. aerospace engineering.

    b. chemical engineering.

    c. bioengineering.

    d. civil engineering.

17. _____ is the application of science to solve an everyday problem.

18. Draw Conclusions Insulation is a product that keeps cool air inside a house when it is hot outside and heat inside when it is cold outside. How does this product benefit society?

_____

_____

_____

APPLY THE BIG ? How does technology affect society?

19. Think of a technology that you frequently use. Describe three ways that this technology has affected society and the environment.

_____

_____

_____

_____

_____

_____

_____

_____

_____

_____

Standardized Test Prep

Multiple Choice

Circle the letter of the best answer.

1. Look at the graph. What can you predict about the sale of DVD recorders after 2008?

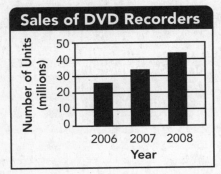

Sales of DVD Recorders

   A   No DVD recorders will be sold in 2009.
   B   People will buy DVD recorders forever.
   C   People will buy DVD recorders until a new technology better meets their needs.
   D   The number of DVD recorders sold will not be affected by emerging technology.

2. A dishwasher is an example of a technological system. What is an input of a dishwasher?

   A   Dishes are cleaned.
   B   Water sprays the dishes.
   C   Soap is put in.
   D   The dishwasher turns off.

3. A jacket made of a new, lightweight material has just been designed. Which of the following prototypes would be the best one to use to test how comfortable the jacket is to wear?

   A   a computer model of the jacket
   B   a miniature version of the jacket
   C   a full-sized version of the jacket, made of cotton
   D   a full-sized version of the jacket, made of the new material

4. Engineers have designed a new car. Which of the following trade-offs would have a negative impact on public safety?

   A   choosing low-cost materials over good results in crash tests
   B   choosing appearance over comfort
   C   choosing a better music system over a better air conditioning system
   D   choosing a more powerful engine over better gas mileage

5. A new robotic vacuum cleaner that was developed this year is an example of

   A   an obsolete technology.
   B   an emerging technology.
   C   a construction technology.
   D   a communication technology.

Constructed Response

Use your knowledge of science to help you answer Question 6. Write your answer on a separate sheet of paper.

6. Use the picture above to describe a system. First, name the parts of the bicycle that make up the system. Then, describe how these parts contribute to input, process, output, and feedback.

TENSION IN ALL THE
RIGHT
PLACES

Model It Use straws, rubber bands, and paper clips to model a tensegrity structure. Use the straws as beams, elastic bands to provide tension, and paperclips to hold the elastic bands to the ends of the straws.

Rock stars and football players play to huge crowds at the world-famous Georgia Dome. But what really makes the Georgia Dome legendary is that it's the largest cable-supported domed stadium in the world! A cool engineering idea called tensegrity gave engineers the inspiration for its famous domed roof.

A tensegrity structure spreads out tension and compression along all of its parts. In the Georgia Dome, three oval hoops sit high above the ground, held in place by vertical steel posts and a horizontal system of steel cable triangles. The steel posts push down on the corners of the cable triangles while the triangles pull on the posts. This constant compression and tension keeps the strong, lightweight fiberglass roof up. You can compare it to a giant, very stable umbrella!

Tensegrity structures use very little material to cover a lot of space, so they can be very cost-effective. They are also incredibly strong and flexible. If outside pressure becomes too strong, the Georgia Dome's roof will shift to reduce tension in certain areas, while maintaining the overall tension.

Rain or shine, the Georgia Dome's famous roof will be around for a long time, thanks to its inventive structure.

Museum of Science

ENGINEERING SOLUTIONS

There is no such thing as a typical day for Lisa Short. As a chemical engineer for the United States government, Lisa uses her knowledge of biochemistry to improve the way new medications are developed. Some days she may build, and install, equipment in a biotechnology lab. Or you might find Lisa researching better, faster, and less expensive techniques for producing medications. Other days Lisa works in the lab, analyzing data from experiments.

In high school, Lisa focused on science and math. In college, she majored in chemical engineering, where she learned how to set up experiments, used lab equipment, and studied chemistry and biochemistry. Today she uses that knowledge to improve technology for making medications.

Chemical engineers work in factories, labs, or offices. They work to improve processes and tools for making products from raw materials. These products include medications, cleaning products, paints, cosmetics, and just about anything else that is made by combining ingredients to create a new substance. They are problem solvers who use chemistry to improve how things work. So next time you use soap or hand lotion, or watch someone fill a vehicle with gasoline, realize that a chemical engineer worked to make these products better.

Chemical engineers use laboratory equipment, such as the centrifuge shown here. A centrifuge separates solid or liquid particles in a mixture.

Research It Chemical engineers use chemistry to improve materials. Identify a problem you have experienced with a material that does not do what it is supposed to do. (One example might be plastic wrap that doesn't cling tightly enough.) Write a letter to the company describing the problem and stating how the product should be improved.

Safety Symbols

These symbols warn of possible dangers in the laboratory and remind you to work carefully.

 Safety Goggles Wear safety goggles to protect your eyes in any activity involving chemicals, flames or heating, or glassware.

 Lab Apron Wear a laboratory apron to protect your skin and clothing from damage.

 Breakage Handle breakable materials, such as glassware, with care. Do not touch broken glassware.

 Heat-Resistant Gloves Use an oven mitt or other hand protection when handling hot materials such as hot plates or hot glassware.

 Plastic Gloves Wear disposable plastic gloves when working with harmful chemicals and organisms. Keep your hands away from your face, and dispose of the gloves according to your teacher's instructions.

 Heating Use a clamp or tongs to pick up hot glassware. Do not touch hot objects with your bare hands.

 Flames Before you work with flames, tie back loose hair and clothing. Follow instructions from your teacher about lighting and extinguishing flames.

 No Flames When using flammable materials, make sure there are no flames, sparks, or other exposed heat sources present.

 Corrosive Chemical Avoid getting acid or other corrosive chemicals on your skin or clothing or in your eyes. Do not inhale the vapors. Wash your hands after the activity.

 Poison Do not let any poisonous chemical come into contact with your skin, and do not inhale its vapors. Wash your hands when you are finished with the activity.

 Fumes Work in a well-ventilated area when harmful vapors may be involved. Avoid inhaling vapors directly. Only test an odor when directed to do so by your teacher, and use a wafting motion to direct the vapor toward your nose.

 Sharp Object Scissors, scalpels, knives, needles, pins, and tacks can cut your skin. Always direct a sharp edge or point away from yourself and others.

 Animal Safety Treat live or preserved animals or animal parts with care to avoid harming the animals or yourself. Wash your hands when you are finished with the activity.

 Plant Safety Handle plants only as directed by your teacher. If you are allergic to certain plants, tell your teacher; do not do an activity involving those plants. Avoid touching harmful plants such as poison ivy. Wash your hands when you are finished with the activity.

 Electric Shock To avoid electric shock, never use electrical equipment around water, or when the equipment is wet or your hands are wet. Be sure cords are untangled and cannot trip anyone. Unplug equipment not in use.

 Physical Safety When an experiment involves physical activity, avoid injuring yourself or others. Alert your teacher if there is any reason you should not participate.

 Disposal Dispose of chemicals and other laboratory materials safely. Follow the instructions from your teacher.

 Hand Washing Wash your hands thoroughly when finished with an activity. Use soap and warm water. Rinse well.

 General Safety Awareness When this symbol appears, follow the instructions provided. When you are asked to develop your own procedure in a lab, have your teacher approve your plan before you go further.

Using a Laboratory Balance

The laboratory balance is an important tool in scientific investigations. You can use a balance to determine the masses of materials that you study or experiment with in the laboratory.

Different kinds of balances are used in the laboratory. One kind of balance is the triple-beam balance. The balance that you may use in your science class is probably similar to the balance illustrated in this Appendix. **To use the balance properly, you should learn the name, location, and function of each part of the balance you are using. What kind of balance do you have in your science class?**

The Triple-Beam Balance

The triple-beam balance is a single-pan balance with three beams calibrated in grams. The back, or 100-gram, beam is divided into ten units of 10 grams each. The middle, or 500-gram, beam is divided into five units of 100 grams each. The front, or 10-gram, beam is divided into ten units of 1 gram each. Each of the units on the front beam is further divided into units of 0.1 gram. What is the largest mass you could find with a triple-beam balance?

The following procedure can be used to find the mass of an object with a triple-beam balance:
1. Place the object on the pan.
2. Move the rider on the middle beam notch by notch until the horizontal pointer on the right drops below zero. Move the rider back one notch.
3. Move the rider on the back beam notch by notch until the pointer again drops below zero. Move the rider back one notch.
4. Slowly slide the rider along the front beam until the pointer stops at the zero point.
5. The mass of the object is equal to the sum of the readings on the three beams.

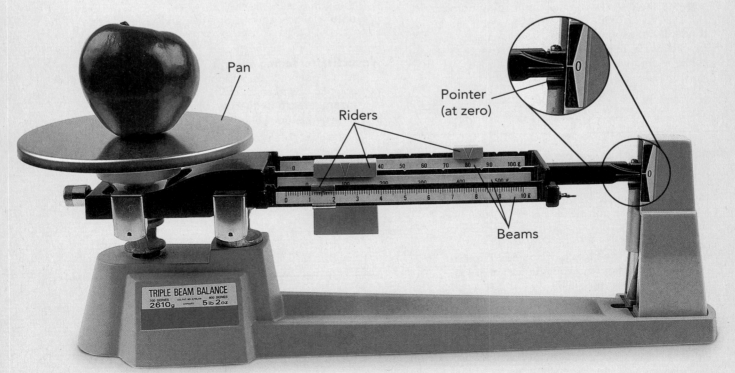

Pan

Riders

Pointer (at zero)

Beams

TRIPLE BEAM BALANCE
700 SERIES   U.S. PAT. NO. 3,733,234   800 SERIES
2610g   CAPACITY   5 lb 2 oz

GLOSSARY

A

accuracy How close a measurement is to the true or accepted value. (82)
exactitud Cuán cerca está una medida del valor verdadero o aceptado.

aerospace engineering The branch of engineering that consists of the design, construction, and testing of airplanes and spacecraft. (142)
ingeniería aeroespacial Rama de la ingeniería que consiste en diseñar, construir y poner a prueba aviones y naves espaciales.

anomalous data Data that do not fit with the rest of a data set. (86)
datos anómalos Información que no encaja con los otros datos de un conjunto de datos.

B

benefit A good consequence of taking an action. (40)
beneficio Buena consecuencia de una acción.

bioengineering The branch of engineering that involves applying engineering principles to biology and medicine. (142)
bioingeniería Rama de la ingeniería que consiste en aplicar los principios de la ingeniería a la biología y la medicina.

brainstorming A process in which group members freely suggest any creative solutions that come to mind. (127)
lluvia de ideas Proceso mediante el cual los miembros de un grupo sugieren libremente cualquier solución creativa que se les ocurre.

C

chemical engineering The branch of engineering that deals with the conversion of chemicals into useful products. (143)
ingeniería química Rama de la ingeniería que trata de la conversión de las sustancias químicas en productos útiles.

civil engineering The branch of engineering that includes the design and construction of roads, bridges, and buildings. (143)
ingeniería civil Rama de la ingeniería que incluye el diseño y la construcción de caminos, puentes y edificios.

classifying The process of grouping together items that are alike in some way. (8)
clasificar Proceso de agrupar objetos con algún tipo de semejanza.

constraint Any factor that limits a design. (128)
restricción Cualquier factor que limita un diseño.

controlled experiment An experiment in which only one variable is manipulated at a time. (22)
experimento controlado Experimento en el cual sólo se manipula una variable a la vez.

controversy A public disagreement between groups with different views. (49)
controversia Desacuerdo público entre grupos con diferentes opiniones.

cost A negative result of either taking or not taking an action. (40)
costo Resultado negativo de una acción o de la falta de acción.

cultural bias An outlook influenced by the beliefs, social forms, and traits of a group. (13)
prejuicio cultural Opinión influenciada por las creencias, costumbres sociales y características de un grupo.

D

data Facts, figures, and other evidence gathered through observations. (23)
dato Hechos, cifras u otra evidencia reunida por medio de observaciones.

deductive reasoning A way to explain things by starting with a general idea and then applying the idea to a specific observation. (15)
razonamiento deductivo Manera de explicar las cosas en la que se aplica una idea general a una observación específica.

density The measurement of how much mass of a substance is contained in a given volume. (76)
densidad Medida de la masa de una sustancia que tiene un volumen dado.

E

Earth and space science The study of Earth and its place in the universe. (54)
ciencias de la Tierra y el espacio Estudio de la Tierra y su lugar en el universo.

electrical engineering The branch of engineering that involves the design of electrical systems, including power, control systems, and telecommunications. (143)
ingeniería eléctrica Rama de la ingeniería que se dedica al diseño de los sistemas eléctricos, como los sistemas de electricidad, control y telecomunicación.

engineer A person who uses both technological and scientific knowledge to solve practical problems. (119)
ingeniero Persona capacitada para usar conocimientos tecnológicos y científicos para resolver problemas prácticos.

engineering The application of science to satisfy needs or solve problems. (141)
ingeniería Aplicar las ciencias para satisfacer necesidades o resolver problemas.

estimate An approximation of a number based on reasonable assumptions. (81)
estimación Aproximación de un número basada en conjeturas razonables.

ethics The rules that enable people to know right from wrong. (12)
ética Reglas que le permiten a una persona reconocer lo que es moral y lo que no lo es.

evaluating Comparing observations and data to reach a conclusion about them. (8)
evaluar Comparar observaciones y datos para llegar a una conclusión.

evidence Observations and conclusions that have been repeated. (43)
evidencia Observaciones y conclusiones que se han repetido.

experimental bias A mistake in the design of an experiment that makes a particular result more likely. (13)
prejuicio experimental Error en el diseño de un experimento que aumenta la probabilidad de un resultado.

F

feedback Output that changes a system or allows the system to adjust itself. (94)
retroalimentación Salida que cambia un sistema o permite que éste se ajuste.

field Any area outside of the laboratory. (104)
campo Cualquier área fuera del laboratorio.

G

goal Purpose. (122)
meta Propósito.

graph A picture of information from a data table; shows the relationship between variables. (89)
gráfica Representación visual de la información de una tabla de datos; muestra la relación entre las variables.

H

hypothesis A possible explanation for a set of observations or answer to a scientific question; must be testable. (20)
hipótesis Explicación posible de un conjunto de observaciones o respuesta a una pregunta científica; se debe poder poner a prueba.

I

inductive reasoning Using specific observations to make generalizations. (16)
razonamiento inductivo Usar observaciones específicas para hacer generalizaciones.

inferring The process of making an inference, an interpretation based on observations and prior knowledge. (6)
inferir Proceso de hacer una inferencia; interpretación basada en observaciones y conocimientos previos.

input Material, energy, or information that goes into a system. (94)
entrada Material, energía o informacion que se agrega a un sistema.

International System of Units (SI) A system of units used by scientists to measure the properties of matter. (71)
Sistema Internacional de Unidades (SI) Sistema de unidades que los científicos usan para medir las propiedades de la materia.

L

life science The study of living things, including plants, animals, and microscopic life forms. (53)
ciencias de la vida Estudio de los seres vivos como plantas, animales y formas de vida microscópicas.

GLOSSARY

linear graph A line graph in which the data points yield a straight line. (90)
gráfica lineal Gráfica en la cual los puntos de los datos forman una línea recta.

M

making models The process of creating representations of complex objects or processes. (9)
hacer modelos Proceso de crear representaciones de objetos o procesos complejos.

manipulated variable The one factor that a scientist changes during an experiment; also called independent variable. (21)
variable manipulada Único factor que el científico cambia durante un experimento; también llamada variable independiente.

mass A measure of how much matter is in an object. (73)
masa Medida de cuánta materia hay en un cuerpo.

mean The numerical average of a set of data. (85)
media Promedio numérico de un conjunto de datos.

mechanical engineering The branch of engineering that deals with the design, construction, and operation of machinery. (143)
ingeniería mecánica Rama de la ingeniería que trata del diseño, la construcción y la operación de máquinas.

median The middle number in a set of data. (85)
mediana Número del medio de un conjunto de datos.

meniscus The curved upper surface of a liquid in a column of liquid. (74)
menisco Superficie superior curva de un líquido en una columna de líquido.

metric system A system of measurement based on the number 10. (71)
sistema métrico Sistema de medidas basado en el número 10.

mode The number that appears most often in a list of numbers. (85)
moda Número que aparece con más frecuencia en una lista de números.

model A representation of a complex object or process, used to help people understand a concept that they cannot observe directly. (93)
modelo Representación de un objeto o proceso complejo que se usa para explicar un concepto que no se puede observar directamente.

N

nonlinear graph A line graph in which the data points do not fall along a straight line. (90)
gráfica no lineal Gráfica lineal en la que los puntos de datos no forman una línea recta.

O

objective Describes the act of decision-making or drawing conclusions based on available evidence. (14)
objetivo Describe el acto de tomar una decisión o llegar a una conclusión basándose en la evidencia disponible.

observing The process of using one or more of your senses to gather information. (5)
observar Proceso de usar uno o más de tus sentidos para reunir información.

obsolete No longer in use. (120)
obsoleto Que ya no está en uso.

opinion An idea about a situation that is not supported by evidence. (43)
opinión Idea sobre una situación que la evidencia no sustenta.

output Material, energy, result, or product that comes out of a system. (94)
salida Material, energía, resultado o producto que un sistema produce.

P

patent A legal document issued by a government that gives an inventor exclusive rights to make, use, or sell an invention for a limited time. (131)
patente Documento legal emitido por el gobierno que otorga a un inventor los derechos exclusivos de hacer, usar o vender un invento por un tiempo limitado.

percent error A calculation used to determine how accurate, or close to the true value, an experimental value really is. (84)
error porcentual Cálculo usado para determinar cuán exacto, o cercano al valor verdadero, es realmente un valor experimental.

personal bias An outlook influenced by a person's likes and dislikes. (13)
prejuicio personal Perspectiva influenciada por las preferencias de un individuo.

physical science The study of energy, motion, sound, light, electricity, magnetism, and chemistry. (55)
ciencias físicas Estudio de la energía, el movimiento, el sonido, la luz, la electricidad el magnetismo y la química.

precision How close a group of measurements are to each other. (82)
precisión Cuán cerca se encuentran un grupo de medidas.

predicting The process of forecasting what will happen in the future based on past experience or evidence. (7)
predecir Proceso de pronosticar lo que va a suceder en el futuro, basándose en evidencia o experiencias previas.

process A sequence of actions in a system. (94)
proceso Secuencia de acciones en un sistema.

prototype A working model used to test a design. (129)
prototipo Modelo funcional usado para probar un diseño.

Q

qualitative observation An observation that deals with characteristics that cannot be expressed in numbers. (5)
observación cualitativa Observación que se centra en las características que no se pueden expresar con números.

quantitative observation An observation that deals with a number or amount. (5)
observación cuantitativa Observación que se centra en un número o cantidad.

R

range The difference between the greatest value and the least value in a set of data. (85)
rango Diferencia entre el mayor y el menor valor de un conjunto de datos.

responding variable The factor that changes as a result of changes to the manipulated, or independent, variable in an experiment; also called dependent variable. (21)
variable de respuesta Factor que cambia como resultado del cambio de la variable manipulada, o independiente, en un experimento; también llamada variable dependiente.

risk-benefit analysis The process of evaluating the possible problems of a technology compared to the expected advantages. (137)
análisis de riesgo y beneficios Proceso por el cual se evalúan los posibles problemas de una tecnología y se compara con las ventajas deseadas.

S

safety symbols A sign used to alert you to possible sources of accidents in an investigation. (101)
símbolos de seguridad Señal de alerta sobre elementos que pueden causar accidentes durante una investigación.

science A way of learning about the natural world through observations and logical reasoning; leads to a body of knowledge. (5)
ciencia Estudio del mundo natural a través de observaciones y del razonamiento lógico; conduce a un conjunto de conocimientos.

scientific inquiry The ongoing process of discovery in science; the diverse ways in which scientists study the natural world and propose explanations based on evidence they gather. (19)
indagación científica Proceso continuo de descubrimiento en la ciencia; diversidad de métodos con los que los científicos estudian el mundo natural y proponen explicaciones del mismo basadas en la evidencia que reúnen.

scientific law A statement that describes what scientists expect to happen every time under a particular set of conditions. (27)
ley científica Enunciado que describe lo que los científicos esperan que suceda cada vez que se da una serie de condiciones determinadas.

scientific literacy The knowledge and understanding of scientific terms and principles required for evaluating information, making personal decisions, and taking part in public affairs. (43)
conocimiento científico Conocimiento y comprensión de los términos y principios científicos necesarios para evaluar información, tomar decisiones personales y participar en actividades públicas.

scientific theory A well-tested explanation for a wide range of observations or experimental results. (27)
teoría científica Explicación comprobada de una gran variedad de observaciones o resultados de experimentos.

GLOSSARY

significant figures All the digits in a measurement that have been measured exactly, plus one digit whose value has been estimated. (82)
cifras significativas En una medida, todos los dígitos que se han medido con exactitud, más un dígito cuyo valor se ha estimado.

skepticism An attitude of doubt. (12)
escepticismo Actitud de duda.

subjective Describes the influence of personal feelings on a decision or conclusion. (14)
subjetivo Describe la influencia de sentimientos personales sobre una decisión o conclusión.

system A group of related parts that work together to perform a function or produce a result. (94)
sistema Grupo de partes relacionadas que trabajan conjuntamente para realizar una función o producir un resultado.

T

technology How people modify the world around them to meet their needs or to solve practical problems. (117)
tecnología Modo en que la gente modifica el mundo que la rodea para satisfacer sus necesidades o para solucionar problemas prácticos.

trade-off An exchange in which one benefit is given up in order to obtain another. (128)
sacrificar una cosa por otra Intercambio en el que se renuncia a un beneficio para obtener otro.

troubleshooting The process of analyzing a design problem and finding a way to fix it. (130)
solución de problemas Proceso por el cual se analiza un problema de diseño y se halla una forma de solucionarlo.

V

variable A factor that can change in an experiment. (21)
variable Factor que puede cambiar en un experimento.

volume The amount of space that matter occupies. (74)
volumen Cantidad de espacio que ocupa la materia.

W

weight A measure of the force of gravity acting on an object. (73)
peso Medida de la fuerza de gravedad que actúa sobre un cuerpo.

INDEX

Page numbers for key terms are printed in **boldface** type.

A

Accuracy, 82
time measurement, 79
Aerospace engineering, 142
Anomalous data, 85
Application of skills
Apply It!, 13, 14, 17, 21, 41, 45, 51, 59, 91, 95, 104, 122, 128, 137, 141
Do the Math!, 107
calculate, 55, 76, 84, 134
estimate, 81
explain, 81
graph, 7
infer, 7
interpret data, 7, 55, 134
interpret photos, 81
predict, 23, 76
read graphs, 23
Interactivities, 14, 47, 49, 53, 71, 72, 74, 78, 82, 85, 129, 130, 136
Science Matters
Bakelite: Molding the Future, 64
Caffeine Causes Hallucinations!, 65
Engineering Solutions, 151
Ready for a Close-Up, 33
Smallpox on the Loose, 111
Tension in All the Right Places, 150
When We Think We Know But It Isn't So, 32
You Lost What?!, 110
Apply It! *See* Application of skills
Assessment
Assess Your Understanding, 9, 13, 17, 20, 26, 27, 41, 43, 45, 47, 51, 55, 57, 59, 71, 79, 83, 87, 89, 91, 93, 95, 99, 104, 105, 119, 121, 123, 131, 133, 136, 139, 141, 143, 145
Review and Assessment, 29–30, 61–62, 107–108, 147–148
Standardized Test Prep, 31, 63, 109, 149
Study Guide, 28, 60, 106, 146
Astrophysicist, 54

B

Benefit
cost-benefit analysis, **40**
risk-benefit analysis, **137**
Bias, 13
awareness of, 13, 32
controlling, 22

Big Idea, xx–xxi
Big Question
Answer the Big Question, 26, 47, 87, 136
Apply the Big Question, 30, 62, 108, 148
chapter opener, 1, 35, 67, 113
Explore the Big Question, 26, 47, 86, 136
Review the Big Question, 28, 60, 106, 146
Unlock the Big Question, 4, 10, 18, 38, 42, 48, 52, 70, 80, 88, 92, 100, 116, 124, 132, 140
Bioengineering, 142
Biomedical researcher, 53
Brainstorming, 127

C

Careers in science, 52–59
astrophysicist, 54
biomedical researcher, 53
chemical engineer, 151
chemist, 55
in earth and space science, **54**
engineer, 119
entomologist, 53
fisheries scientist, 53
geoscientist, 54
hydrologist, 54
impact on non-science careers, 58–59
in life science, **53**
in physical science, **55**
physical science technician, 55
physics teacher, 55
robotics, 52
science filmmaker, 33
and teamwork, 56–57
Carson, Rachel, 50
Celsius (C), 78
Centimeter (cm), 72
Chemical Engineer, 151
Chemical engineering, 143
Chemist, 55
Civil engineering, 143
Classifying, 8
Clocks, 79
Coexisting technologies, 121
Communication
of scientific results, 25
of technological solutions, 131
Complex systems, 98–99
Constraint (technological design), 128
Consumer information, 39, 65
Controlled experiment, 18, 22

Controversy, scientific, 49–51
Cost, 40
Creativity, 11
Cubic centimeter (cm^3), 74
Cultural bias, 13
Curiosity, 10, 11
Current technologies, 120

D

Data, 23
Decision-making
consumer and citizen issues, 39–41, 65
cost-benefit analysis, **40**
risk-benefit analysis, **137**
using technology wisely, 137–139
Deductive reasoning, 15
Density, 76
of common substances, 77
Designing
experiments, 21–26
technological solutions, 127–128
Did You Know?, 15, 39, 75, 135
Digital Learning
Apply It!, 11, 39, 45, 59, 91, 95, 105, 123, 137, 141
Art in Motion, 135, 136
Do the Math!, 21, 53, 73, 81, 85, 135
Interactive Art, 9, 16, 26, 27, 49, 58, 59, 85, 87, 89, 97, 117, 125
My Reading Web, 2, 3, 36, 37, 68, 69, 114, 115
My Science Coach, 9, 13, 17, 19, 20, 26, 27, 29, 41, 43, 45, 47, 51, 55, 57, 59, 61, 71, 73, 79, 83, 87, 89, 91, 93, 95, 97, 99, 101, 104, 105, 107, 119, 121, 123, 131, 133, 136, 137, 139, 141, 143, 145, 147
Planet Diary, 4, 5, 10, 11, 18, 19, 38, 39, 42, 43, 48, 49, 52, 53, 70, 71, 80, 81, 88, 89, 92, 93, 100, 101, 116, 117, 124, 125, 132, 133, 140, 141
Real-World Inquiry, 47, 142, 143
Untamed Science, xx, 1, 34, 35, 66, 67, 112, 113
Virtual Lab, 5, 8, 21, 24, 71
Vocab Flash Cards, 3, 37, 69, 115
Do the Math! *See* Application of skills

INDEX

Page numbers for key terms are printed in **boldface** type.

E

Earth science, **54**
Einstein, Albert, 48
Electrical engineering, **143**
Emerging technology, 121
Engineer, **119**
Engineering, **141**–145, 150
   aerospace, **142**
   benefits of, 144–145
   bioengineering, **142**
   chemical, **143**
   civil, **143**
   electrical, **143**
   mechanical, **143**
Entomologist, 53
Environmental issues
   consequences of technology, 64,
   134, 136
   in controversial discoveries, 50
   and plastic, 64
   recycled material, 38
   saving energy, 145
Estimate, **81**
Ethics, **12**
Evaluating, **8**
   information, 42–47
Evidence, **43**
Experiment, controlled, 18, **22**
   collecting and interpreting data,
   23
   communicating results, 25
   controlling bias, 22
   controlling variables, 21–22
   designing, 22, 26
   drawing conclusions, 24
Experimental bias, **13,** 22

F

Faulty reasoning, 17
Feedback
   in scientific systems, **94**
   in technological systems,
   122–123
Field, **105**
Filmmaker, scientific, 33
Fisheries scientist, 53

G

Galileo Galilei, 18, 49
Geoscientist, 54

Goal

   of technological systems,
   122–123
   of technology, 117, 119
Goodall, Jane, 4
Gram (g), **73**
Grams per cubic centimeter
   (g/cm^3), **76**
Grams per milliliter (g/mL), 76
Graphs, 88–91
   line, 89
   linear, **90**
   nonlinear, **90**

H

Honesty, **11**
Hydrologist, 54
Hypothesis, **20**

I

Inductive reasoning, **16**
Industrial Revolution technology,
   133
Inferring, **6**
Information Age technology, **133**
Input
   in scientific systems, **94**
   in technological systems,
   122–123
Inquiry, scientific, **19**
Inquiry Skills. *See* Science Inquiry
   Skills; Science Literacy Skills
Interactivities. *See* Application of
   skills
International System of Units. *See*
   SI (International System of Units)
Inventions, 64, 116, 124, 132, 140,
   150
Iron Age technology, **133**
Irregular solids, volume of, 74–75

K

Kelvin (K), **78**
Kilogram (kg), **73**
Kilometer (km), **72**

L

Lab Zone
   Inquiry Warm-Up, 4, 10, 18, 38,

   42, 48, 52, 70, 80, 88, 92, 100,
   116, 124, 132, 140
   Lab Investigation, 26, 57, 91,
   123
   Quick Lab, 9, 13, 17, 20, 27, 41,
   43, 45, 47, 51, 55, 59, 71, 79, 83,
   87, 89, 93, 95, 99, 104, 105, 119,
   121, 131, 133, 136, 139, 141,
   143, 145
Latimer, Lewis H., 116
Law, scientific, **27**
Length, measuring, 72
Life science, **53**
Line graphs, 89
Linear graphs, **90**
Liquid volume, 74
Liter (L), **74**

M

Making models, **9**
Manipulated variables, **21**
Mass, measuring, **73**
Materials for technological
   design, 127
Math. *See* Application of skills
Mathematics, 80–87
   accuracy and precision, **82**
   calculating percent error, **84**
   estimation, **81**
   mean, median, mode, and
   range, **85**
   reasonable and anomalous
   data, 85
Mean, **85**
Measurement, 70–79, 110
   adding, subtracting, and
   multiplying, 83
   density (grams per milliliter or
   cubic centimeter), **76**–77
   of earthquakes, 80
   length (meter), 72
   mass (kilogram), **73**
   metric system, **71**
   SI (International System of Units),
   71–79
   standard, 71
   temperature (Celsius or Kelvin),
   78
   time (second), 79
   volume (liter/cubic centimeter),
   74–75
Measurement units
   Celsius, 78
   centimeter (cm), 72
   cubic centimeter (cm^3), 74
   gram (g), 73

grams per cubic centimeter (g/cm^3), 76
grams per milliliter (g/mL), 76
Kelvin, 78
kilogram (kg), 73
kilometer (km), 72
liter (L), 74
meter (m), 72
milligram (mg), 73
millimeter (mm), 72
second (s), 79
Mechanical engineering, 143
Median, 85
Meniscus, 74
Meter (m), 72
Metric system, 71
Milligram (mg), 73
Millimeter (mm), 72
Mode, 85
Models, 92, **93**
making, **9**
of systems, 96–99
My Planet Diary
Biography, 4, 116
Blog, 140
Careers, 52
Disaster, 100
Discovery, 10, 80, 124
Fun Facts, 38, 42, 70, 92, 132
Misconceptions, 18
Science Stats, 88
Voices From History, 48

N

Nonlinear graphs, 90

O

Objective reasoning, 14
Observing, 5, 32
Obsolete technology, 120
Open-mindedness, 12
Opinion, 43
Output
of scientific systems, **94**
of technological systems, 122–123

P

Patent, 131
Percent error, 84
Personal bias, 13

Physical science, 55
technician, 55
Physics teacher, 55
Precision, 82
Predicting, 7
from models, 96
Process
of scientific systems, **94**
of technological systems, 122–123
Process Skills. *See Science Inquiry Skills; Science Literacy Skills*
Prototype, 129

Q

Qualitative observation, 5
Quantitative observation, 5

R

Range, 85
Reading Skills
reading/thinking support strategies
apply concepts, 13, 15, 27, 57, 58, 59, 82, 94, 95, 101, 107, 119, 123, 144
define, 17, 41, 51, 121
describe, 87, 99
estimate, 81
explain, 13, 20, 51, 54, 74, 81, 93, 99, 131, 136, 139
identify, 16, 21, 45, 56, 57, 58, 78, 79, 89, 91, 95, 98, 119, 128, 142
interpret diagrams, 78, 97
interpret maps, 9
interpret photos, 81
interpret tables, 24, 79
list, 95, 104, 131
make generalizations, 45, 62, 104, 108
make judgments, 105, 108, 145, 147
mark text, 13, 23, 46, 54, 84, 90, 94, 131, 138, 144
name, 26, 71
read graphs, 23, 90
review, 47, 59, 83, 91, 105, 123, 145
target reading skills
ask questions, 5, 11, 54
compare and contrast, 9, 29, 40, 73, 91, 107, 147
identify the main idea, 54, 94, 131

relate cause and effect, 13, 17, 84, 141, 144, 147
relate text and visuals, 90, 120
sequence, 23, 49, 79, 122, 147
summarize, 12, 43, 99, 103, 139
Reasonable and anomalous data, 85
Reasoning
deductive, **15**
faulty, 17
inductive, **16**
objective, **14**
subjective, **14**
Responding variables, 21
Risk-benefit analysis, 137
Robotics, 52

S

Safety, 100–105, 111
accident response, 105
in the field, 104
in the lab, 100–103, 111
preparation, 101
through technology and engineering, 135, 144
Safety symbols, 101
Science, 5
branches of, 52–59
earth and space science, **54**
life science, **53**
physical science, **55**
robotics, 52
and society, 38–59
becoming an informed consumer and citizen, 38–41, 65
careers in science, 52–57
controversial discoveries, 48–51, 64
finding and evaluating information, 42–47
impact on work, 58–59
and technology, 119
Science Inquiry Skills
basic process skills
calculate, 55, 71, 72, 76, 83, 84, 85, 107, 134
classify, 8, 9, 14, 56, 118, 122, 143, 147
communicate, 10, 18, 25, 30, 38, 42, 50, 59, 80, 88, 119, 121, 128, 135
design solutions, 127, 128
graph, 7

INDEX

Page numbers for key terms are printed in **boldface** type.

infer, xx, 6, 7, 29, 34, 47, 53, 56, 58, 77, 117, 121, 131, 143, 145
make models, 17, 96, 102
measure, 72, 73, 107
observe, 5, 6, 29, 104
predict, 7, 23, 29, 51, 76, 91
work with design constraints, 128
experimental methods
analyze experimental results, 86
analyze sources of error, 24, 44, 107
evaluate data reliability, 46, 61
identify experimental bias, 44
technology design/evaluation
analyze costs and benefits, 40, 61, 133, 137, 138, 148
build a prototype, 129
evaluate the impact on society, 41, 62, 136
evaluate models and systems, 123
identify a need, 125
research the problem, 126
troubleshoot, 130

Science Literacy Skills
demonstrate consumer literacy, 139
distinguish evidence and opinion, 43
evaluate science in the media, 62
evaluate scientific claims, 45, 61
identify faulty reasoning, 17
integrated process skills
control variables, 21
design experiments, 22, 26, 77, 87
develop hypotheses, 20, 66, 112
draw conclusions, 21, 29, 59, 104, 134, 137, 148
form operational definitions, 76
interpret data, 7, 45, 55, 83, 91, 134, 148
pose questions, 19, 39, 41, 57, 61

Science Matters. *See* Application of skills

Scientific attitudes, 10–13
awareness of bias, 13, 32
curiosity, honesty, and creativity, 10–11
open-mindedness and skepticism, 12
strong sense of ethics, 12
teamwork, 56–57

Scientific inquiry, 19
designing and conducting experiments, 21–26
developing hypotheses, 20
posing questions, 19
Scientific law, 27
Scientific literacy, 43–45
Scientific reasoning
deductive, **15**
faulty, 17
inductive, **16**
objective vs. subjective, 14
Scientific skills, 5–9
classifying, **8**
evaluating, **8**
inferring, **6**
making models, **9, 91**
observing, 4, **5**, 32
predicting, **7**
Scientific theory, 27
Scientific tools
graphs, 88–91
mathematics, 80–87
measurement, 70–79
models, 92–99
Scientists. *See* Careers in science
Semmelweis, Ignaz, 50
SI (International System of Units), 71–79
cubic meter (volume), 74–75
kelvin (temperature), 78
kilogram (mass), 73
kilograms per cubic meter (density), 76–77
meter (length), 72
newton (force), 73
prefixes, 71
second (time), 79
Significant figures, 82
Simple systems, 97
Skepticism, 12
Society
and science, 38–59
becoming an informed consumer and citizen, 38–41, 65
careers in science, 52–57
controversial discoveries, 48–51, 64
finding and evaluating information, 42–47
impact on work, 58–59
and technology, 132–139
consequences, 134–135
impact, 132–133, 136
using wisely, 136–139
Solids, volume of, 74–75
Space science, 54

Stone Age technology, 133
Subjective reasoning, 14
Systems, 94–99
complex models, 98–99
simple models, 97

T

Technology, 117–139, 150
steps, 124–131
build a prototype, 129
communicate the solution, 131
design a solution, 127–128
identify the need, 125
research the problem, 126
troubleshoot and redesign, 130
goal of, 117, 119, **122**–123
progress of, 120–121
social impact, 132–139
systems, 122–123
Temperature, measuring, 78
Theory, scientific, 27
Thermometer, 78
Time, measuring, 79
Trade-offs
technological design, **128**
value of technology, 138
Troubleshooting, 130

U

Understanding by Design. *See* Big Question

V

Variables, 21
Vocabulary Skills
identify multiple meanings, 68, 104
identify related word forms, 2, 25
use context to determine meaning, 36, 46, 114, 138
Volume, measuring, 74–75

W

Watches, 79
Weight, 73

ACKNOWLEDGMENTS

Staff Credits

The people who made up the *Interactive Science* team—representing composition services, core design digital and multimedia production services, digital product development, editorial, editorial services, manufacturing, and production—are listed below.

Jan Van Aarsen, Samah Abadir, Ernie Albanese, Bridget Binstock, Suzanne Biron, MJ Black, Nancy Bolsover, Stacy Boyd, Jim Brady, Katherine Bryant, Michael Burstein, Pradeep Byram, Jessica Chase, Jonathan Cheney, Arthur Ciccone, Allison Cook-Bellistri, Rebecca Cottingham, AnnMarie Coyne, Bob Craton, Chris Deliee, Paul Delsignore, Michael Di Maria, Diane Dougherty, Kristen Ellis, Theresa Eugenio, Amanda Ferguson, Jorgensen Fernandez, Kathryn Fobert, Julia Gecha, Mark Geyer, Steve Gobbell, Paula Gogan-Porter, Jeffrey Gong, Sandra Graff, Adam Groffman, Lynette Haggard, Christian Henry, Karen Holtzman, Susan Hutchinson, Sharon Inglis, Marian Jones, Sumy Joy, Sheila Kanitsch, Courtenay Kelley, Chris Kennedy, Toby Klang, Greg Lam, Russ Lappa, Margaret LaRaia, Ben Leveillee, Thea Limpus, Dotti Marshall, Kathy Martin, Robyn Matzke, John McClure, Mary Beth McDaniel, Krista McDonald, Tim McDonald, Rich McMahon, Cara McNally, Melinda Medina, Angelina Mendez, Maria Milczarek, Claudi Mimo, Mike Napieralski, Deborah Nicholls, Dave Nichols, William Oppenheimer, Jodi O'Rourke, Ameer Padshah, Lorie Park, Celio Pedrosa, Jonathan Penyack, Linda Zust Reddy, Jennifer Reichlin, Stephen Rider, Charlene Rimsa, Stephanie Rogers, Marcy Rose, Rashid Ross, Anne Rowsey, Logan Schmidt, Amanda Seldera, Laurel Smith, Nancy Smith, Ted Smykal, Emily Soltanoff, Cindy Strowman, Dee Sunday, Barry Tomack, Patricia Valencia, Ana Sofia Villaveces, Stephanie Wallace, Christine Whitney, Brad Wiatr, Heidi Wilson, Heather Wright, Rachel Youdelman

Photography

All uncredited photos copyright © 2011 Pearson Education.

Cover, Front and Back
J. I. Alvarez-Hamelin, M. Beiró, L. Dall'Asta, A. Barrat, A. Vespignani;
http://xavier.informatics.indiana.edu/lanet-vi/
http://sourceforge.net/projects/lanet-vi/

Front matter
Page vi, NASA Human Spaceflight Collection; **vii,** Eric Rorer/Aurora/Getty Images; **viii,** Dan Guravich/Photo Researchers/Getty Images; **ix,** Christian Darkin/Photo Researchers, Inc.; **xi,** iStockphoto.com; **xiii girl,** JupiterImages/Getty Images; **xvi,** iStockphoto.com; **xviii chimps,** Manoj Shah/The Image Bank/Getty Images; **xix l,** Comstock/JupiterUnlimited; **xix r,** Kevin Fleming/Corbis.

Chapter 1
Pages xxii–1, NASA Human Spaceflight Collection; **3 t,** Michael Nichols/National Geographic Image Collection; **3 m,** Ken Seet/Corbis; **3 m bkgrnd,** Jon Helgason/iStockphoto.com; **3 b,** Richard Haynes; **4,** Michael Nichols/National Geographic Image Collection; **5,** Karl Ammann/Nature Picture Library; **6 b,** Manoj Shah/The Image Bank/Getty Images; **6 t,** Anup Shah/Nature Picture Library; **7,** Christoph Becker/Nature Picture Library; **8,** Kennan Ward/Corbis; **9,** Rainer Raffalski/Alamy; **10 bkgrnd,** Jennifer Borton/iStockphoto.com; **10 b,** Sarah Holmstrom/iStockphoto.com; **11 tl,** Stephen Dalton/Photo Researchers, Inc.; **11 bl,** Karin Lau/iStockphoto.com; **11 r,** Kurt Lackovic/Alamy; **12,** Photo Network/Alamy; **13 peanut,** Gary Woodard/iStockphoto.com; **14 girl,** Ken Seet/Corbis; **14–15 spread,** Jon Helgason/iStockphoto.com; **15 children,** MBI/Alamy; **15 t,** Duncan Walker/iStockphoto.com; **15 b,** Jon Helgason/iStockphoto.com; **16–17,** Stephen Dorey-Commercial/Alamy; **17,** Redmond Durrell/Alamy; **18,** *Galileo Demonstrating the Law of Gravity of the Free Fall* (detail, *The Trial of Galileo*) (ca. 1839), Giuseppe Bezzuoli. Fresco. Museum of Physics and Natural History (Museo di Fisica e Storia Naturale), Florence, Italy; **19,** Andy Sands/Nature Picture Library; **20,** Richard Haynes; **21 t,** Idamini/Alamy; **22 t,** Idamini/Alamy; **22 b,** Richard Haynes; **23–24,** Idamini/Alamy; **25 b,** Idamini/Alamy; **25 t,** U.S. Department of Energy Human Genome Program http://www.ornl.gov/hgmis/home.shtml; **26 hand and crumpled paper,** D. Hurst/Alamy; **26 unfolded paper,** Don Carstens/Brand X Pictures/JupiterImages; **26 folded paper,** Aartpack; **27,** Photodisc/Getty Images; **28 t,** Karl Ammann/Nature Picture Library; **28 m,** Photo Network/Alamy; **28 b,** Idamini/Alamy; **29,** Renee Stockdale/Animals Animals/Earth Scenes; **30,** Image100/Corbis.

Interchapter Feature
Page 32, Academie des Sciences, Paris/Archives Charmet/The Bridgeman Art Library; **33,** Tiago Estima/iStockphoto.com.

Chapter 2
Pages 34–35, H. Armstrong Roberts/ClassicStock/Corbis; **35 inset,** Comstock/SuperStock; **37 t,** Bob Daemmrich/Corbis; **37 bm,** Eric Rorer/Aurora/Getty Images; **37 b,** Chris Sattlberger/Digital Vision/Getty Images; **38,** Courtesy of Steve Loken; **39,** Larry Dale Gordon/The Image Bank/Getty Images; **40 t,** Bob Daemmrich/Corbis; **40 l,** David Muscroft/Artlife Images; **40 r,** Angela Hampton Picture Library/Alamy; **41 bkgrnd,** Fancy/Veer/Corbis; **41 t,** Vereshchagin Dmitry/Shutterstock; **41 b,** Lisamarie/Dreamstime.com; **42 bkgrnd,** MedicalRF/Photo Researchers, Inc.; **42 b,** Andrew Brookes/Corbis; **43 r,** Daniel Templeton/Alamy; **43 l,** John Short/JupiterImages; **45,** Inspirestock/JupiterImages; **46 browser window,** Haywiremedia/Dreamstime.com; **46–47 bkgrnd,** Imagebroker/Alamy; **48 bkgrnd,** Viorika Prikhodko/iStockphoto.com; **48 l,** Bettmann/Corbis; **49 bkgrnd,** Ekaterina Pokrovskaya/Shutterstock; **49 r,** The Print Collector/age Fotostock; **50 b,** George Silk/Time & Life Pictures/Getty Images; **50–51 t,** James P. Blair/National Geographic/Getty Images; **51,** Stacy Gold/National Geographic/Getty Images; **52,** Copyright © 2009 Phil Channing; **53 t,** Custom Medical Stock Photo, Inc.; **53 bl,** Tony Kurdzuk/Star Ledger/Corbis; **53 br,** Eric Rorer/Aurora/Getty Images; **54 t,** Associated Press/AP Images; **54 m,** Chris Sattlberger/Digital Vision/Getty Images; **54 b,** Nancy Simmerman/Getty Images; **55 b,** Michael Newman/PhotoEdit, Inc.; **55 t,** Stock Connection Blue/Alamy; **55 m,** William Taufic/Corbis; **56 tr,** Radius Images/Alamy; **56 tl,** Friedrich Saurer/Alamy; **56 bl,** NASA/Corbis; **56 br,** Corbis; **57 tr,** Digital Vision/Alamy; **57 tl,** Radius Images/JupiterImages; **57 bl,** Corbis RF/Alamy; **57 br,** Keith Weller/USDA Agricultural Research Service/Bugwood.org; **58 t,** Johnny Franzn/Johner Images Royalty-Free/Getty Images; **58 m,** Maria Grazia Casella/Alamy; **58 b,** Thinkstock/Corbis;

Beak and Test

Beaks.

2 Qualitative.
    Each beak are.   The bird kind
different shape,   of beak angry.

2. Quantitave

    I see 6 beaks.

    There are 6 beak
each beak had each own
different shape and size,

I think bird 1 is seed eater.

    I think 4 is a nectar eater

    I think bird 2 catches meat.
        Qulitative
1 look like an Hawk feet

Each bird have different kind of
    legs.
        Quntive
    The are 24 toes

I think bird
I would gasp prey
3+5 is a first runner.

take note

this space is yours—great for drawing diagrams and making notes

this is your book

you can write in it

this is your book

you can write in it

take note

this space is yours—great for drawing diagrams and making notes

this is your book

you can write in it